Careers
Education
&Guidance

Careers Education & Guidance

A handbook and guide to careers education, guidance and training

Bill Rogers

CRAC

Published by Hobsons Publishing PLC

Acknowledgements

The author and the publisher are most grateful to the teachers, advisers and others who have assisted in the preparation of this book, and especially Carol Mariner, Bolton Careers Service; Mrs C Wright and Ms J Hurst, CISTEL; Mr M Smith, Senior Adviser, City of Sheffield; Mrs M Barnes; Mr B Wilcock; Ms M Byrne; Leigh Careers Support Group; friends and colleagues in Wigan and Leigh schools, colleges, and careers offices; Jeff Engels and Bill Law for their infectious enthusiasm; Joan, Louise and Gareth.

First published 1984

CRAC publications are published under exclusive licence and royalty agreements by Hobsons Publishing PLC. The Careers Research and Advisory Centre is an independent non-profit-making body.

ISBN 0 86021 617 9

R/0.5jj/H/HG

Sometimes the masculine pronoun is used in the text where the reference might more accurately refer to both sexes. This is to avoid tortuous, repetitive sentence structure peppered with 'he or she'. Unless otherwise specified readers should construe the reference 'he' as applying equally to both sexes.

Careers Education and Guidance

Contents

Page

Use of terms in this book	6
Introduction	7
Abbreviations	8

Part 1 Careers in context 9

A	The aims of careers education and guidance	10
B	Definitions	11
C	Careers and the core curriculum	12
D	Changes in education	15
E	The alternatives at 16+	20
F	The economic context	22

Part 2 Careers teachers 31

A	The role of the careers teacher	32
B	Systems	39

Part 3 Careers education 45

A	Designing a careers education programme	46
B	Methods	51
C	Resources	57
D	Pulling it all together	102

Part 4 Careers guidance 117

A	Aims and objectives	118
B	Interviewing and counselling	129
C	Information for careers guidance	135

Part 5 Training 149

Appendices

1	Book lists	155
2	Job search computer program	158
3	Major sources of careers publications	inside back cover

Use of terms in this book

An occupation	– a way in which time is used
A job	– a specific task, not necessarily for reward
Work	– carrying out a task or series of tasks, not necessarily for material reward
Employment	– an occupation which is rewarded by money or other material payments
Learning	– gaining knowledge or skill
Teaching	– imparting knowledge or skill through teacher or student-centred learning strategies
Training	– work-related skill instruction
A student	– a person who is attempting to gain knowledge or skill in the final years of compulsory education, and beyond
Careers education and guidance	– There ought to be no distinction made between these two terms, since guidance is always an educative process. For the sake of close analysis in this book though, group learning experiences intended to meet the *common needs* of students are included under 'careers education', whilst learning experiences intended to meet the *particular needs* of individual students – usually but not always in one-to-one situations – are described as 'careers guidance'. In practice, *careers education* often involves guidance, and *careers guidance* always involves education.

Introduction

This handbook is addressed primarily to newly–appointed careers teachers – many of whom will have had no training or experience specifically designed to prepare them for the task – and for students in training.

It should also be of interest to those responsible for the design and implementation of the curriculum in secondary schools and to more experienced careers and other guidance staff – both as a useful reference source and as an aid in clarifying their own aims.

In the ten years since the Employment and Training Act of 1973, careers education and guidance moved inexorably towards a watershed. On one side lay the 'full employment' placement role ascribed by many to the careers service – and by far too many to the careers teacher. On the other side we see an uncertain terrain where the roles of both careers teacher and careers officer are in urgent need of re-definition.

The summer of 1982 marked that watershed. In that year less than 45% of young people aged 16–19 years were in full-time permanent employment. It is now widely accepted – even allowing for world and domestic cyclical fluctuations – that this is not a temporary phenomenon, but a permanent shift in employment patterns.

Against this background, it is hardly surprising that careers teachers find themselves having to justify their role to colleagues, to anxious parents, and to the children they teach. The task is all the more difficult because of the accelerating rate of change facing careers teachers in terms of shrinking employment opportunities and cuts in higher education courses, at the same time that entry qualifications are rising; and in the form of mushrooming pre-vocational courses and YTS schemes under the new training initiative. Then there are those of us who have to consider the long-term implications for students opting for the Training and Vocational Education Initiative (TVEI) at the end of their third year in the secondary school, and their own particular continuous guidance needs.

Paradoxically, the role of 'careers' as it is understood by those responsible for training careers and guidance staff, and by many experienced careers teachers, has never been as central to the secondary school curriculum.

This book attempts to examine this role within the context of present trends and to outline practical systems, methods and resources by which it may be implemented.

Finally, since there is no substitute for specialist preparation – whether you are about to enter the chalk face or are already at it – you will find outlined the various opportunities available for training, re-training, and skill improvement.

There is a very special satisfaction in helping young people to develop the skills and awareness which will enable them to sort out the kind of person they each wish to become; it is also a very special responsibility and one which has never been more difficult. I hope that this book will help to make the task a little easier. *Bill Rogers*

Abbreviations

APU	Applied Psychology Unit – interest questionnaires
BTEC	Business and Technician Education Council
CASCAID	Careers Advisory Service Computer Aid
CCDU	Counselling and Career Development Unit (Leeds University)
CNAA	Council for National Academic Awards
CGLI	City and Guilds of London Institute
CLCI	Careers Library Classification Index
COIC	Careers and Occupational Information Centre
CFA/CPVE	Career Foundation Award/Certificate of Pre-Vocational Education
CRAC	Careers Research and Advisory Centre
FE	Further Education
FEU	Further Education Curriculum Review and Development Unit
FT	Full Time
DE	Department of Employment
DES	Department of Education and Science
FEIS	Further Education Information Service
Dip HE	Diploma in Higher Education
ECCTIS	Educational Counselling and Credit Transfer Information Service
GIST	Girls Into Science and Technology, a Manchester Polytechnic sponsored project
ICO	Institute of Careers Officers
ITB	Industrial Training Board
JIIG-CAL	Job Ideas and Information Generator – Computer Assisted Learning
LEA	Local Education Authority
MSC	Manpower Services Commission
NACGT	National Association of Careers and Guidance Teachers
NFER	National Foundation for Educational Research
NICEC	National Institute for Careers Education and Counselling
TVEI	Training and Vocational Education Initiative
OU	Open University
ORC	Occupational Research Centre
SCIP	Schools Council Industry Project
UCCA	Universities Central Council on Admissions
YTS	Youth Training Scheme

PART 1

Careers in context

A The aims of careers education and guidance

'Careers education and guidance is not a subject but a process on which a school needs to have a policy. Designated careers teachers, subject specialists, and teachers in their pastoral role should contribute.

Careers education and guidance should help individuals:
- to become interested in and aware of opportunities in education and training, in work, and in adult life generally;
- to understand themselves in relation to these opportunities, their strengths and weaknesses, interests, values, qualifications and circumstances;
- to make informed, reasoned decisions;
- to make transitions, in particular from school to the next stage.

It is necessary to prepare young people to cope with unemployment by developing their personal resources and by informing them about helping agencies and teaching them how to use these. They need knowledge of the labour market, including opportunities outside the formal economy, and they need to be aware of the impact of technology and the changing nature of work.'

Source: DES Discussion Document 1983

Although this document was intended to be a basis for discussion by staff in secondary schools and among those responsible for formulating the curriculum and seeing that it is implemented, it is also an excellent synthesis of the aims to which all informed and experienced careers teachers already subscribe.

These aims contain objectives which are primarily to do with *heightening awareness* and others which are to do with the *acquisition of skills*. This distinction is made in the model of the curriculum presented in Diagram 1 (page 13) under the headings 'Life skills' and 'Awareness of self . . . related to opportunities'.

Throughout the remainder of this book the assumption will be that we are seeking to achieve these aims. If you feel the need to explore the rationale behind these aims, please see the list of recommended reading.

B Definitions

'career(n.) 1. Swift course; impetus. *2. Course or progress through life,* esp. when publicly conspicuous or successful; development and success of party, principle, etc.; *course of professional life or employment, way of making livelihood.* – v.i. Go swiftly or wildly.'

Source: *The New Oxford Illustrated Dictionary*

Ask anybody what they understand by the word 'career' and the odds are that they will come close to one of the two definitions italicised above. Which of the two they tend to identify with will almost certainly depend upon how important the work ethic is to them, consciously or subconsciously. Not so much the Protestant work ethic – that doesn't have much of a hold anymore, if it ever did – but rather the inclination to identify oneself, and others, by one's means of making a livelihood. Status and self-esteem are still largely dependent on the nature of the work we do, or do not do.

Social class, one of the major blockages to economic and social progress in Britain, is still measured by categories of employment. How many child-rearing housewives have found themselves neatly pigeon-holed by the question 'And what does your husband do?' – their own experiences and aspirations dismissed as irrelevant? How many middle-aged men made redundant have suddenly found it almost impossible to retain their normal social contacts because of the embarrassment felt by their friends, and the conversational obsession with the work-place?

There are signs that the narrowness of this definition of 'career' is beginning to be acknowledged, slowly by the older generations, much more rapidly by the young. Careers and other guidance staff have been aware that it is inappropriate for at least a decade. They would tend towards the first of the two definitions, 'course or progress through life'. The other definition – 'course of professional life or employment' – is likely to remain the major component for most people for much of the time, but it has become clear that initial employment, youth training schemes, and further education are the first steps on a course which is uncertain, and has the potential for change.

Careers staff would also point out that there are many things other than employment which give impetus to a person's life: parenthood, vocations, voluntary work, continuing education, constructive leisure, local politics, community involvement and so on.

Part 2 examines the role of the careers teacher more closely, but if one starts with the assumption that they would see their major task as preparing young people for adult life by developing the skills and awareness necessary for them to become self-directing, and especially to enable them to make the transition from school, then one can proceed to look first at the curriculum and changes in education and then at the context of that adult life as it faces our school leavers.

C Careers and the core curriculum

Ever since the 'great debate' on education which got under way in 1977, the secondary school curriculum has undergone repeated scrutiny and appraisal. From the first discussion document – *Educating Our Children* – through the government's proposals – *A Framework For the School Curriculum* – to the inspectorate's response to those proposals – *A View of the Curriculum* – careers education is seen as a necessary part of the common core. Given that almost 50% of schools were seen not to be providing timetabled careers education in fourth and fifth years – *Local Authority Arrangements for the School Curriculum* – and resources even then were very limited, both the government and the inspectorate were circumspect in their recommendations, allowing flexibility as to the method of implementation. *'. . . systematic careers education should begin not later than the third secondary year, and it is normally desirable that it should occupy a specific place in the curriculum'* is how *A Framework For the School Curriculum* saw it.

In the time which has elapsed since the last of those reports was issued, changes in employment, further and higher education and training have effectively thrown the secondary curriculum back into the melting pot. We now have the opportunity to look afresh at what it is we ought to be providing at the secondary level, using these reports and the Schools' Council Red Books as a basis for re-appraisal.

In Diagram 1 (opposite) is presented a *simple* model of what the secondary curriculum ought to be concerned with and the way in which it seems to be developing.

The size of each segment is *not* intended to indicate the proportion of time devoted to those elements contained in the segment. Traditionally, however, we have spent a disproportionate amount of time on cultural transmission, at the expense of skills for learning and for life.

A core curriculum. Who am I? Who might I become?

Diagram 1

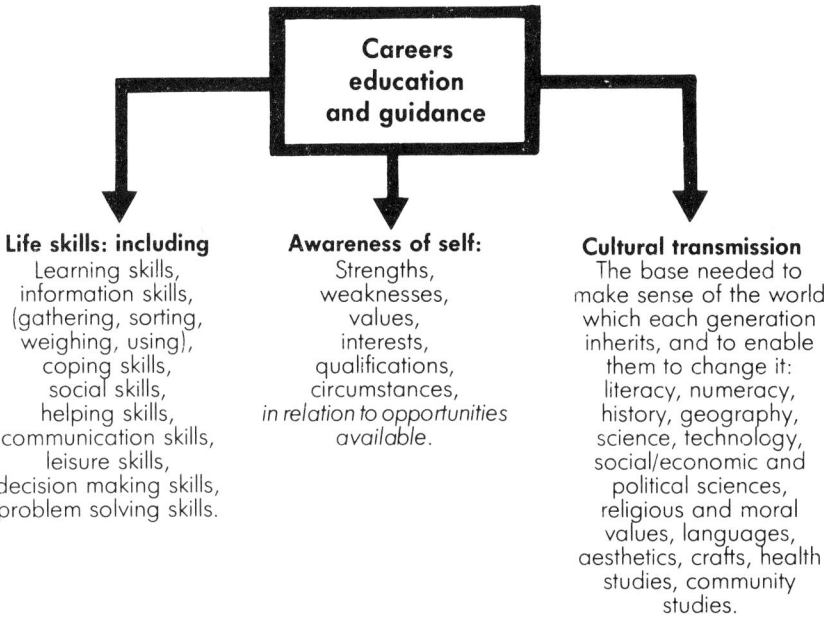

Careers education and guidance

Life skills: including
Learning skills,
information skills,
(gathering, sorting,
weighing, using),
coping skills,
social skills,
helping skills,
communication skills,
leisure skills,
decision making skills,
problem solving skills.

Awareness of self:
Strengths,
weaknesses,
values,
interests,
qualifications,
circumstances,
*in relation to opportunities
available.*

Cultural transmission
The base needed to
make sense of the world
which each generation
inherits, and to enable
them to change it:
literacy, numeracy,
history, geography,
science, technology,
social/economic and
political sciences,
religious and moral
values, languages,
aesthetics, crafts, health
studies, community
studies.

NB Like all simple models, this one requires some explanation. The headings are provided only for the purpose of identification: they should not exist in practice in discrete and separate packages. Life skills – of which self-awareness is clearly a part – should emerge through the way in which cultural transmission occurs. Rather than injecting life skills into the curriculum in the final years of secondary education, we ought to be developing learning strategies which make them implicitly part of all of our teaching programmes. It is partly because they have not been integrated consciously into 'academic' courses that they have become explicit in 'pre-vocational' courses.

Now that so much of our new technology is directed to the provision of information, the accumulation of information through education will be less important than the skills which enable us to select, process and use the available information effectively. The time saved in this way should enable us to explore more fully the creative, aesthetic and social aspects of our personalities. In theory at least, this offers us the opportunity to get back to the basics of secondary education – preparation for adult life and learning – rather than preparing for examinations first and life second.

In preparing children to make the transition from school to training, continuing education, employment and adult life, careers education and guidance has a co-ordinating role in the curriculum. It attempts to relate the importance of the cultural base to future opportunities. It tries to show the importance of life skills to those opportunities. Above all, it helps pupils towards a realistic appraisal of their own developing abilities in relation to the range of opportunities available and prepares them to make their first transition towards adult life and independence.

In the final school years it is not merely a part of the curriculum, it is the integrating core of the curriculum. Under whatever guise or title, it has to appear at the centre of every secondary school curriculum.

> *'The only man who is educated is the man who*
> *has learned how to learn, the man who has*
> *learned how to adapt and change, the man who*
> *has realised no knowledge is secure.'*
>
> Carl Rogers, *Freedom to Learn for the Eighties*

D Changes in education

On the assumption that you are either studying the education system as a student, or have been working in secondary education for some time, you will find outlined only those changes and pressures within secondary and tertiary education and training which have specific implications for careers staff.

Secondary education
11-16

'Falling rolls' The decline in the secondary school population of between 30% and 45% in different authorities, peaking in most cases by the last quarter of this decade, is having the following effects: the contraction of some schools and the closure of others; limited opportunities for staff promotion; re-deployment and almost certain redundancy within the next few years. In some schools this is leading to increasing professionalism and openness to change, in others to retrenchment and disillusionment. On the positive side, more space becomes available and this should be a good time to press for a specialist careers suite, interview rooms, library etc by amending existing rooms at low cost. Unfortunately, in the present economic climate, falling rolls do not mean improved pupil–teacher ratios, increased resources or extra preparation time.

'Economy' means just that. Enlightened LEAs and heads are making extra resources available for careers education and guidance, but in the main you will have to fight as hard as ever for capitation, staffing and time on and off the timetable.

'Accountability' and **'Relevance'** are two criteria being applied in schools and at times working against each other. At no time since the second world war have schools been more subject to scrutiny. Principally because of changes to the structure of governing bodies required by the 1981 Education Act, the publishing of the reports of Her Majesty's Inspectors and of examination results, the pressure on heads and LEAs from parents, the DES and the government is growing. They find themselves having to encourage staff to improve exam results while implementing a more 'relevant' curriculum, which most observers would agree needs to be tied far less to examinations dictated by the specific requirements of higher education. And this at a time of economy.

From the point of view of subject teachers – and heads of departments in particular – these pressures come against the background of falling rolls and limited resources. A decline in the numbers opting for their subject from third year upwards can herald redeployment or redundancy for one of their colleagues.

Under these circumstances, careers teachers need to be tactful, well–informed and well able to argue the case for any expansion of careers on the timetable – either directly or through other subjects – at the expense of other disciplines. Even requests for work experience release may be met with opposition from departments fighting to maintain, or raise, examina-

15

tion results.

On the other hand the cry for 'relevance', correctly interpreted, can give support to careers education and show other disciplines the way forward.

TVEI The Training and Vocational Education Initiative (TVEI) is at present an experiment occurring in only fourteen local education authorities, of which the author's is one. At the time of writing, however, this five year experiment has been extended to cover 46 more such pilot schemes in Wales and England and bids have been invited from Scotland.

TVEI is sure to have a major influence on the 11–16 curriculum and poses considerable guidance problems for careers teachers, as well as opening up opportunities for them to make their teaching more experience based.

The significant aspects of TVEI are as follows:

a It is sponsored by the Manpower Services Commission (MSC) and not by the DES. In this sense it is a new departure in British education. Control, through funding, rests with the Department of Employment rather than the Department of Education.

b It has the primary aim of providing a technical and vocational course geared towards a pre–BTEC model. In this sense it seeks to combine pre-vocational and general education.

c The target group will vary from scheme to scheme but is – in theory at least – the whole ability range, starting at 14 and continuing through to 16 or 18 years of age. In practice, the participating group in the initial stages is almost certainly going to be skewed towards average or below average pupils.

d The key element in all courses will be practical, transferable skill-learning in clusters of job families – manufacturing, marketing, service, for example. A period – or periods – of work experience will be integral to the course.

e Other core elements are likely to include: numeracy, communications, outdoor pursuits and community studies, social and personal development (including careers), periods of directed study and the opportunity to take a limited number of traditional subjects on offer in the rest of the curriculum.

f A system of student profiling and tutoring will be expected on all schemes.

The implications for careers teachers would appear to be:

– having to explain to parents and pupils during the third year at secondary school the alternatives presented by TVEI and the more traditional courses, and the extent to which they may diverge or converge at later stages in respect of further education and employment opportunities

– ensuring that part of the guidance and profiling process is related to vocational development

– ensuring from the outset that everybody involved – parents, pupils, staff and employers – are aware that this is a pre-vocational course of

education intended to improve learning skills and capability, and not a job-tasting and job training exercise
- providing careers education and guidance as part of the course, and taking advantage of the experiential parts of the course – especially the skill learning, work experience, leisure and community studies – to reinforce teaching and guidance.

The sixth form . . . is undergoing considerable change. The 'new sixth' of the 1970s with its mix of courses is feeling the impact of high youth unemployment and MSC–sponsored schemes. Repeat O–levels, CSEs and other general courses are understandably less attractive to students now that inflated qualifications and competition have reduced their market value. A–levels and vocational courses in more buoyant personal service sectors retain their appeal, but the latter are far more common in FE institutions. The pre-voc course has rapidly gained ground and the new Career Foundation Award/Certificate for Pre-Vocational Education is intended primarily for schools and sixth form colleges. For many students, however, the alternative presented by YTS – employment–based education and training with pay, with 40%–60% chance of employment at the end of it – may be a more attractive and a more realistic proposition. The result of that could be a reversion to the academic sixth with some BTEC (see FE below) courses for TVEI students, and others, who may have access to a YTS placement integrated into their course. Much will depend upon the development of YTS and changes in higher education reflected in post–16 academic courses.

Further education institutions are going through a similar period of adjustment. BEC and TEC courses – examinations validated by the Business and Technician Education Council – are a mainstay among the vocational courses and represent an alternative to A–levels for entry to commerce and industry at 18, and to higher diploma and degree courses. Other vocational courses and many part-time and day release courses have suffered contraction in areas of declining manufacturing employment. Pre-vocational courses and the servicing of the educational component of YTS seemed to offer scope for expansion, but the reluctance of the MSC to sanction education–based schemes at 16+, and its encouragement of employers to undertake the whole of the scheme themselves, has left some authorities with excess capacity in their FE institutions. Considerable flexibility is having to be shown in meeting student demand, at very short notice.

Higher education establishments have experienced well–publicised cuts and are continuing to operate economies and search for means of supplementing their income. The main effects and other trends are:
- greater competition for entry and higher conditional offers from the universities, polytechnics and colleges at A–level
- a reduction in the number and range of courses offered, especially in social sciences and some specialised technologies
- a dramatic fall in provision of initial teacher training at the secondary

level, with a rise in places for junior/primary school training
- moves to restrict entry onto PGCE – Post Graduate Certificate of Education courses – according to annual supply needs, and to bar graduates in certain disciplines from entry
- there is a possibility that a system of student loans may be introduced to supplement the existing mandatory grants
- serious consideration is being given to a structure of two–year general degrees, followed by optional vocationally–based certificates of one or more years' duration.

Until falling rolls work their way through to higher education, the task of motivating students and of being realistic about the advantages of what used to be called 'deferred gratification' – putting off the immediate reward of employment or paid training in favour of possible advantages coming from higher qualifications – will continue to be a difficult one. Sadly, children from working class homes which have not had previous contact with higher education are likely to be the first to suffer from these trends.

YTS: the Youth Training Scheme: The salient points are:

a It is a part of the New Training Initiative, an overall strategy covering all post–16 youth and adult training needs.

b It is controlled by the MSC, overseen by the Youth Training Board, and approved and monitored locally by area manpower boards.

c It is a comprehensive, all–embracing scheme of training for young people. Initially, it offers 48 weeks of paid training – 13 weeks of which should consist of relevant education in literacy, numeracy, manual dexterity, computer literacy and information technology—and life and social skills to the appropriate level.

d At the outset it was seen as a 'permanent bridge from school to work' (Norman Tebbit, Employment Secretary). Athough confined at present to 16-year olds, and some 17– and 18–year olds, the intention was that it should eventually cover all school–leavers. Already many employers have merged their existing apprenticeship programmes with the scheme.

e Although there are three modes of provision – mode A: employer–based; mode B1: LEA and voluntary schemes, community projects, training workshops etc; mode B2: FE–based work skills courses – the MSC favours employer–based schemes and this is clearly the way in which the scheme will develop.

f Employers, colleges, local authorities and private consultancies can apply to become managing agencies for the scheme.

g Employers can recruit directly from the pool of school leavers, although the majority will go through the careers service.

h The principle of 'additionality' means that the MSC will fund two trainees whom a firm would normally have recruited, provided that it will take on extra trainees (normally three) under the scheme. This suggests that somewhere in the region of 40% of mode A–based trainees may be retained in employment or training at the end of their YTS year by their MSC A 'employer'. Clearly the percentage will differ widely from firm to firm and industry to industry.

i The MSC intends that continuous assessment of performance and profiling should take place. It is mandatory that a YTS certificate be provided at the end of the course, outlining occupational achievements, experience gained, additional achievements and experience in other learning opportunities.

The implications of YTS for schools:

Inasmuch as this scheme was designed to cater for all school–leavers – other than those entering higher education – YTS has major implications for schools, and for careers teachers in the following areas:
- learning and assessment
- life and social skills
- earlier definition of special needs
- the link between FE and schools
- the link between schools and industry
- pressure on school–based work experience schemes as YTS takes priority on placements and training time
- the whole curriculum
- vocational guidance, in the fifth year in particular.

The alternatives at 16+

The cumulative effect of changes which have already taken place in employment, education and training on the alternatives facing our fifth year school leavers is shown in diagram 2 (page 21).

The most significant change is the contraction of direct employment opportunities and the expansion of youth training. With the exception of those firms recruiting directly for specific apprenticeship–linked schemes, the bulk of careers guidance regarding YTS will be to do with job families. In the MSC's report – 'Training for Skill Ownership' – now translated into a guidebook, employers are asked to try to relate their training to the Occupational Training Families – OTFs – listed overleaf.

However long it takes for this training strategy to be fully implemented, it does at least present a coherent if arbitrary basis for identifying employment sectors.

There are also obvious links with the TVEI job families. It is important to note, however, that the concepts of transferability of these skills to other sectors within families has been questioned and it is essential that training should include variety of work experience.

The difficult area for guidance, which is very much in a transitional phase, is the pattern of transfer from continuing education into employment or training. One of the dilemmas facing guidance staff is whether students of average ability opting for academic courses at 16 (and here are included non–YTS pre-vocational courses) will miss out on employment opportunities if the YTS scheme really does become the permanent bridge to employment. This could be the same dilemma which faced students who found themselves too old for apprenticeships after one year in the sixth form.

OTF no	Occupation	Key purpose
1	Administrative, clerical and office services	Information–processing
2	Agriculture, horticulture, forestry and fisheries	Nurturing and gathering living resources
3	Craft and design	Creating single or small numbers of objects using hand/power tools
4	Installation, maintenance and repair	Applying known procedures for making equipment work
5	Technical and scientific	Applying known principles to making things work/usable
6	Manufacturing and assembly	Transforming metallic and non-metallic materials through shaping, constructing, and assembling into products
7	Processing	Intervening into the working of machines when necessary
8	Food preparation and service	Transforming and handling edible matter
9	Personal service and sales	Satisfying the needs of individual customers
10	Community and health services	Meeting socially–defined needs of the community
11	Transport services	Moving goods and people

Within the next five years the patterns at all age levels should become clear; in the meantime it will always be a matter for individual guidance and decision making, and it will be the teachers' responsibility to see that they and their pupils are as well informed as possible. Part 2 will indicate ways in which this can be achieved.

E The alternatives at 16+

a Enter employment full time
b Join the Youth Training Scheme ⟨ work experience / work preparation
c Undertake remedial education to enhance employment and life prospects
d General education for personal development and pre-employment preparation
e Undertake a vocational course
f Undertake a non-vocational course.

The implications of these changes for the careers teacher

Increasingly you will find yourself responsible for the education and guidance of children with a wider range of individual differences, including educationally, mentally and physically disadvantaged pupils (see pages 145–7) – all of whom will face:

a A delay in entry into employment, with a longer transitional period of further education and training

b A contraction in employment opportunities, and a changing pattern of employment.

c An increasing premium placed on educational attainment *and* on proven 'capability' during pre-vocational and vocational training

d Opportunities for leisure, recurrent education, and training and time spent on non-employment roles, far beyond anything experienced in modern history.

Far from seeing these as problems, you and your pupils have to take them on as challenging opportunities – which in fact they are. Inasmuch as they represent an evolving adult life, your role is to ensure that each of your pupils is sufficiently informed, aware, industrious, flexible and armed with the skills to enable them to respond to opportunities as they present themselves. It is up to the politicians and the rest of us to see that those opportunities develop.

Diagram 2 Alternatives at 16+

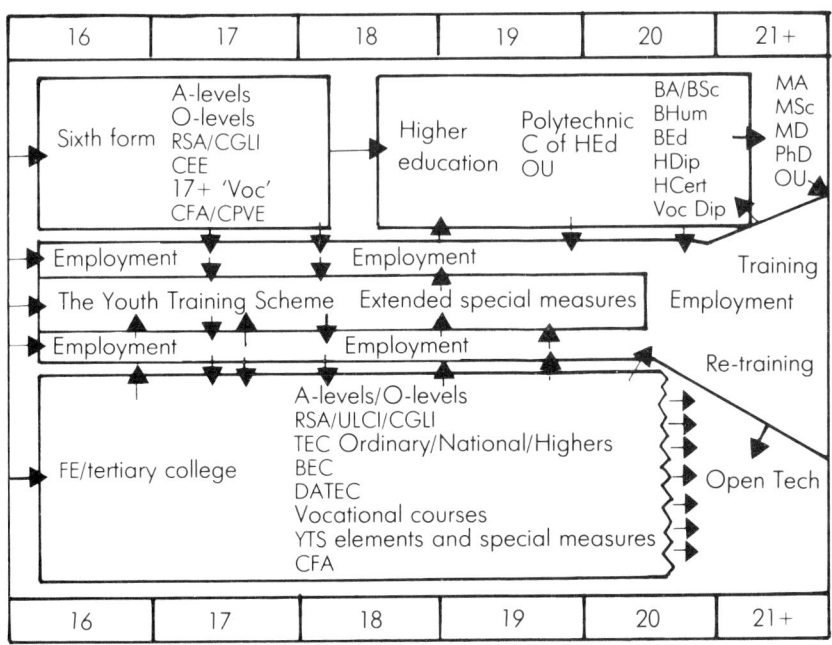

F The economic context

What do our school–leavers do after they have left us? What are the changes taking place in the structure of employment in Britain? How are these changes affecting the role of careers education and guidance? The answers to these questions underpin all the chapters which follow.

1 16–19s (Participation in work, education or unemployment, 1973/74–1981/82)

Diagram 3

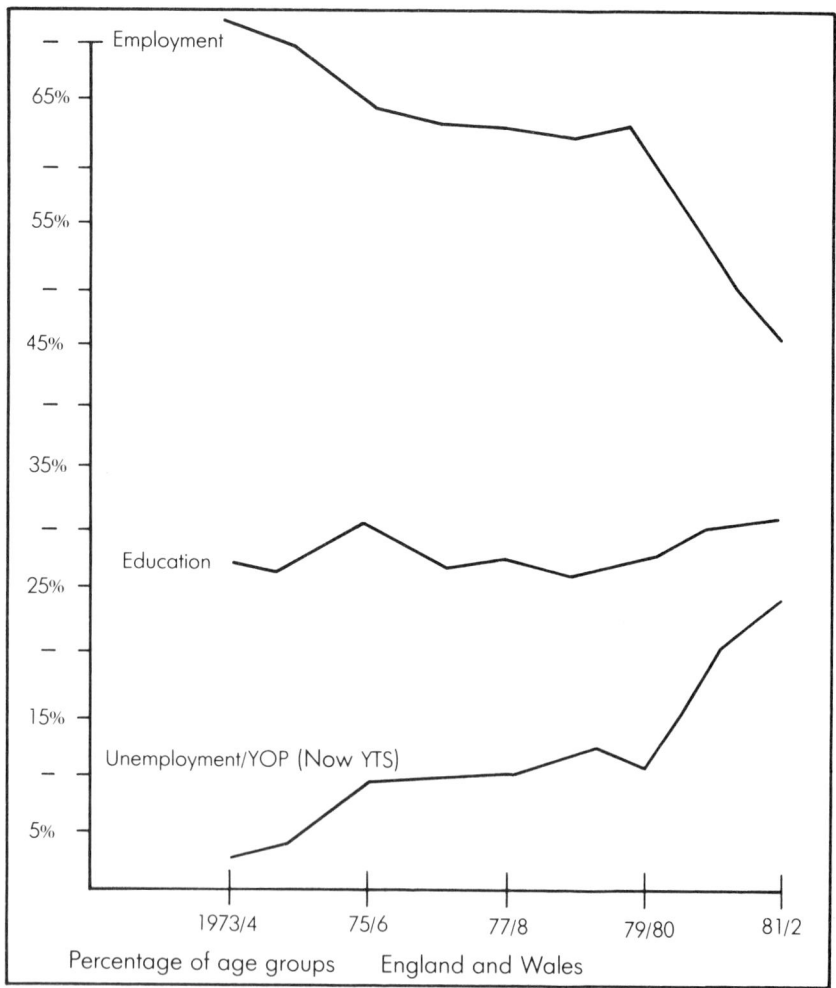

Percentage of age groups   England and Wales

Source: DES Statistical Bulletin 2/83: *Educational and Economic Activity of Young People Aged 16–19 years, in England and Wales from 1973–74 to 1981–82*

The graph in diagram 3 covers the full age range, and highlights the major trends. Included among those unemployed are young people engaged on work experience or training under the YOP schemes. The main results of the survey other than those evident from this graph are as follows:

– 31% of 16–year–old leavers were in full-time school education
– 18% of 16–year–old leavers were in full-time further education
– 28% of 16–year–old leavers were in employment
– 10% of 16–year–old leavers were on YOP schemes
– 14% of 16–year–old leavers were registered as unemployed
– About 80% of 16–year–old leavers were expected to have experienced some form of education or training during 1981/82.
– More girls than boys continued in full-time education at 16.
– Girls seldom obtain employment with part-time day release study.

NB All of these estimates were based upon counts in January or during the autumn term, and therefore only reflect the situation at one point during the year. They relate only to 16–year–old school-leavers in England and Wales.

These trends, together with the expansion of training schemes under the new training initiative, have meant that for many regions of the United Kingdom considerably less than 25% of our 16–year–old school leavers enter permanent employment and around 40% opt for full-time education, with the remainder embarking on youth training schemes.

2 The changing structure of employment

Youth unemployment is but part of a dramatic increase in unemployment as a whole and it is important to take a brief look at the causes of unemployment. There are three basic causes: cyclical, political and structural.

a **Cyclical unemployment** is that which results from swings in demand for goods and services within an economy. World trade, relative price levels, and the expectations of investors tend to determine the duration of these cycles. During the 19th and early 20th centuries the average duration of these cycles was about ten years from peak to peak, with high prices and high employment at the peak; low prices and low employment at the trough. Since the 1960s rising expectations of living standards and full employment policies tended to keep prices and employment high, even during troughs in the trade cycle, and the phrase 'stagflation' – inflation coupled with low growth – was born.

b **Political unemployment** is the result of government intervention, designed to influence other economic indicators, which causes unemployment to rise – directly or indirectly – beyond the level which market forces would dictate. Actions by successive governments to reduce inflation could come under this heading.

c **Structural unemployment** can result from permanent – as opposed to cyclical – changes in market demand. As new products appear and new methods of production are innovated, those sectors of the economy which are unable to compete, or to innovate themselves, will become redundant and their labour force unemployed. Those sectors which are able to innovate will almost certainly do so by adopting new technologies which will save labour costs, improve productivity and increase unemployment.

Our current level of unemployment is the result of a combination of all three causal factors. World trade has been in a trough as the less developed countries struggle with poverty, and mounting international debts and high prices generated in the northern countries, while developed countries in the north face high oil and commodity prices, high interest rates and intense competition. At home the fight against inflation and the drive for higher productivity have left their mark on employment levels.

The important element in all of this is that part which is the result of structural change in the economy. This part alone is not reversible. New opportunities will certainly develop, but many have gone forever and there will be more to follow. That much of it is due to Britain's unique position as the first industrial nation, and the most conservative, is borne out by the following table.

Table 1: Trends in industry 1979 to 1982 (second quarter)

Percentage changes in	Total employed labour force	Manufacturing employment
UK	−9	−20
USA	+2	−10
West Germany	−1	−4
Japan	+3	+3
France	−4	−8
Italy	−3	−1

Some of the differences can be explained by varying political strategies to cushion the impact of unemployment, but it is particularly interesting that those economies which have made the greatest use of new technologies have experienced the smallest decline in employment levels, and in Japan the level of employment actually rose during this period.

Both the UK and the USA have had a similar determination to reduce inflation and it is fair to extrapolate that the deficit in manufacturing employment between the UK and the rest of these countries is primarily the result of structural changes. Obsolete plant, overmanning, adherence to outdated methods and products, inadequate technical education, poor management and labour relations, have been among the factors responsible for a steady decline in our manufacturing competitiveness dating from the last quarter of the nineteenth century. The world slump, cheap imports and new technologies have simply conspired to bring home more forcibly what economists and historians have been saying for decades. **Technological change** has a specific impact within this process. The potential for change represented by bio-technology is immense – particularly in the field of biological and genetic engineering. Already there are working processes producing chemicals and animal and human foodstuffs from small biochemical 'soups'. Work on animal and plant genetics, and on the prevention and treatment of disease, is accelerating. The full impact here – and in alternative sources of fuel – may be several decades off, but in microelectronic technology the effect on employment, and on work patterns, is already significant.

Microelectronic technology can displace jobs in a number of ways. Jenkins and Sherman in *Leisure Shock* (Eyre Methuen, 1980) identified three areas in which this tends to occur:

a In manufacturing industry the introduction of robotics is, via the 'robo-gate system', displacing skilled repetitive tasks – simple assembly operations, welding, painting and spraying – and material-carrying. A Japanese–owned firm has a fully–automated plant which operates unmanned throughout the weekend and which is capable of working an unmanned night shift in the manner described by Jenkins and Sherman. Small and medium sized companies are now able to afford and use microcomputers to ensure optimum production control and materials handling. The resultant shortening of waiting and delivery times and reduction of stockpiling is labour saving for the innovating firm and creates unemployment in the less go–ahead competitor firms.

b The change from electromechanical components to integrated circuitry and from multi-wire assembly to the use of silicon chips is a second way in which jobs can be lost. Across the whole field of consumer– and capital–goods electronics, fewer parts have to be assembled, produc-tion processes are shortened and, since integrated circuitry is both less likely to break down and easier to replace, fewer maintenance workers will be required.

c In the office, the use of word processors and allied computers has so far tended to modify the nature of the task rather than displace large numbers of clerks and copy– and audio–typists. By the end of this decade, however, it is likely that integrated systems of word processors, working through the telecommunications networks, will have had a major impact on numbers of filing clerks, typists, clerical staff and postmen. Already the Post Office has announced higher profits and productivity with fewer staff – and this even before alternative systems begin to bypass them altogether. Even higher level management posts are at risk, particularly where administrators are resistant to the use of information technology, since it can be designed to bypass them.

A summary of the estimated results of structural change on patterns of employment

a A rapid decline in the number of jobs requiring few skills. Between 1971 and 1978 600,000 such jobs disappeared and it has been estimated that a further million will have gone by 1985.

b Non-manual jobs will soon outnumber manual jobs.

c There will continue to be a decline in the number employed in the manufacturing sector relative to those employed in the service sector.

d A rapid decline in industry and sector specific skills, especially coal, cotton, steel and shipbuilding.

The balance sheet (NB This is a medium–term estimate. In the long run much will depend upon world trade patterns and domestic political strategies. For detailed estimates see Warwick University Institute of Employment Research, 1983 Review of the economy and employment.)

Losses	Little change	Gains
Industrial crafts	Professional/advisory	Computer–based
Retailing	Clerical grades in industry	employment
Mechanical operators	and commerce	Health and welfare
Secretarial grades	Personal services	Manufacture of electronic
Local and central	Vocational education and	devices
government (clerical)	training	Senior management
Manual	School teaching	Information systems
		Security professions
		Engineers and scientists
		Leisure provision
		Recurrent education

If world trade improves and the UK moves into a higher growth solution to economic problems, this will create jobs in the column of 'gains' but accelerate the decline of those in the 'losses' column. Low levels of growth relative to our competitors would simply reduce our competitiveness still further, increase redundancies and limit opportunities for employment in new products and new markets. In either case, it is expected that there will be less paid employment relative to the potential work force, well into the foreseeable future.

Governments, employers and unions are well aware of the implications of this fall in the 'norm' level of employment. Already solutions are being suggested and some of them attempted. There will still be a majority of adults in work at any one time but a sizeable minority will not be. In order to maximise employment opportunities – since the work ethic and employment–generated income play such a central role in our lives – the following strategies are being applied, and will be increased during this decade:

a **Job sharing:** Initial attempts to encourage job-sharing have not been as successful as was hoped. The fact that these were voluntary and generally confined to female workers at a time when many of their husbands felt insecure about the permanence of their own jobs, has certainly contributed to the reluctance of many women to accept an arrangement which in other circumstances they would find congenial. Given a measure of job security, and the necessary income sharing, many of us – male and female alike – would welcome the opportunity to work more efficiently for a shorter period of time and have more time to devote to family, leisure pursuits and personal development.

b **Shorter periods at work:** One of the phenomena of the 'three–day week' during the winter of 1973/4 was the fact that output fell by only 10% even though time spent at work had fallen by 40%. With reduction of overtime and enforced short–time working during slumps, it has become apparent to employers that there is a significant diminishing productivity in the seven extra hours per week which British workers spend at work, as compared with their counterparts abroad.

A 35–hour week would be one solution. Three days a week, 12 hours a day is another method adopted by some companies; four days at 10 hours a day by others.

Longer annual holidays and sabbatical periods have been common abroad and involve the employment of replacement staff.

c **A shorter working life:** This can be achieved by delaying entry into the labour force and/or by lowering the age of retirement. In the UK both strategies are emerging. In the first instance, youth unemployment is causing school leavers to opt for continuing education of one sort or another, or entry to one of the MSC's youth training schemes. At the other end of the scale, there has been only limited legislation – the job release scheme for example – but some firms, and local and central government, have been quick to encourage early retirement as part of their response to requirements to cut manpower and costs, and as an alternative to redundancies. Now that spending cuts are biting harder the process is slowing, but the pressure for earlier retirement will continue to grow.

To summarise the changing pattern of employment

a Quite apart from cyclical unemployment, there has been a permanent fall in the level of full employment as we have come to understand it. In future, fewer people will be required to produce the goods and services which we require.

b Some occupations which school leavers have traditionally entered are no longer going to exist. Where they do exist, opportunities are greatly restricted, levels of entry have risen and competition is considerable.

c New areas of employment are emerging and will continue to do so.

d A high level of education is likely to be required for many of the new or expanding employment opportunities.

e The age of entry to full–time paid employment has effectively risen for most young people.

f Time spent at work is likely to fall and there will be longer periods of training, re-training and between jobs.

g The average school leaver will be likely to change his or her job far more often in a working lifetime.

h The age of retirement is likely to come down and so the working life will be shorter.

i Leisure and other unpaid activities will form a more important and substantial part of our lives.

j Just to complicate matters, the decline in both the birth rate and the death rate in recent years means that the population is ageing. A smaller potential work force will have to support a proportionately larger dependant population, especially now that the birth rate is showing signs of rising again.

k Periods of employment are likely to be interspersed with periods of recurrent education.

The two following diagrams attempt to compare the traditional career pattern, which has been both a conscious and subconscious model for career planning for most of this century, with one of a number of emerging career patterns which clearly reflect the changing employment structure outlined above.

In diagram 4 (below) the traditional age of entry to employment for manual unskilled and semi-skilled workers was the year of completion of compulsory education. For semi-skilled and skilled workers there was a period of apprenticeship ending at around 21. Many workers remained on that grade and completing more or less the same task for the remainder of their working lives, which ended at 65 for men and 60 for women. There was some opportunity for upward movement from these grades, dependent upon part-time or evening study, but upward mobility was the exception rather than the norm.

Diagram 4 A traditional career pattern (male)

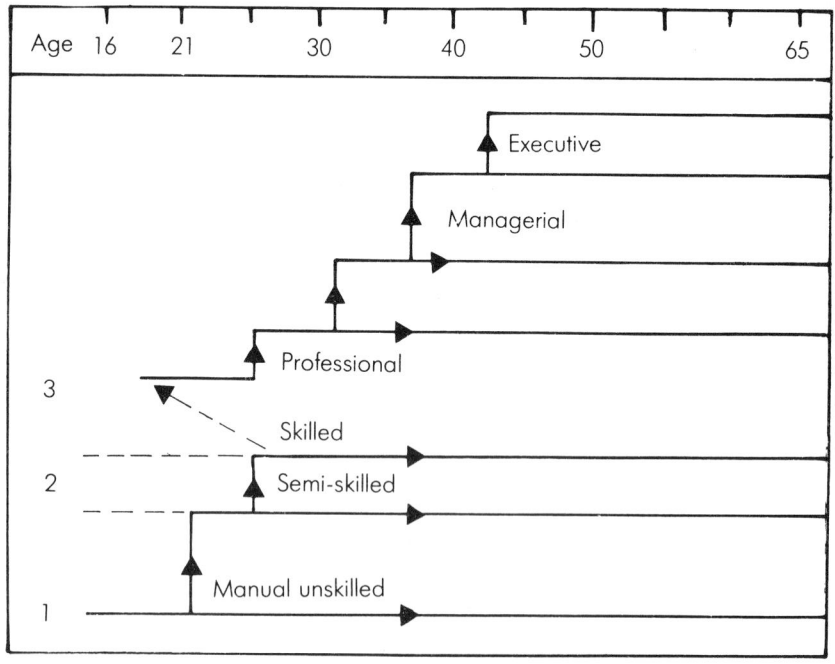

Diagram 5 An emerging career pattern (male and female)

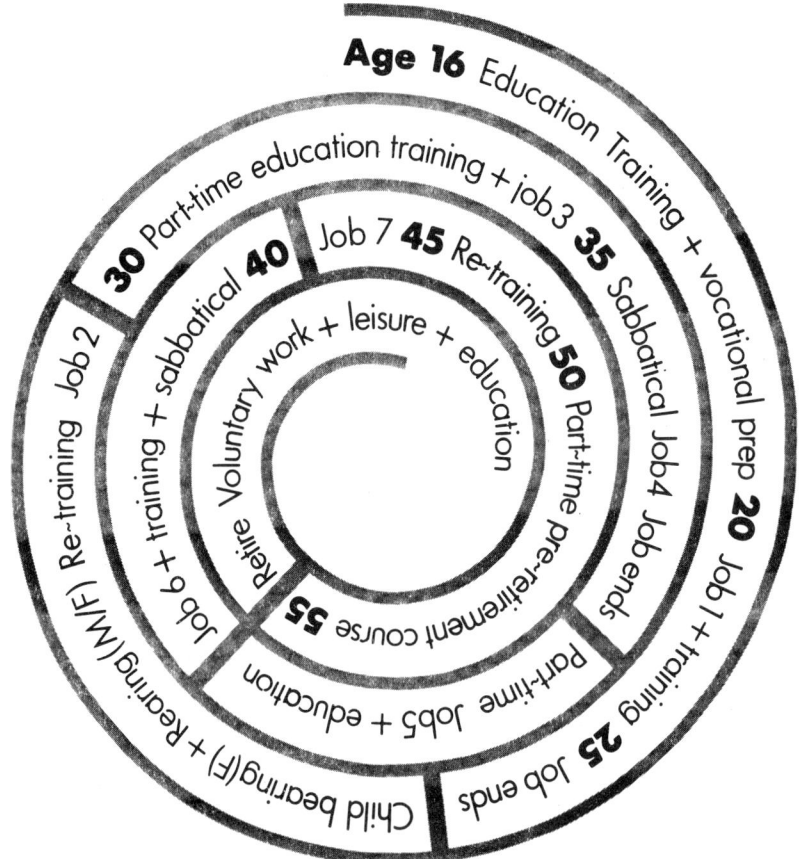

Age 16 Education Training + vocational prep 20 Job 1 + training 25 Job ends Part-time Job 5 + education Child bearing (F) + Rearing (M/F) Re-training Job 2 30 Part-time education training + job 3 35 Sabbatical Job 4 Job ends Part-time pre-retirement course 55 Part-time Job 5 + education Retire Voluntary work + leisure + education 50 Re-training 45 Job 7 40 sabbatical + training + Job 6

Entry to professional grades came generally at 18 or 21 years of age, or at least after several years of voluntary education. Final professional status came after a period of proven worth; promotion and advancement was expected of, and by, the majority. Various cut–off points operated dependent upon ability, ambition, influence and luck. Once the limits of advancement had been reached it was a matter of working through to retirement.

In diagram 5 (above) we see a circular or spiral model. As a one–dimensional circle it represents a continuous cyclical process of education, training, work, education and so on, without implying any vertical advancement in terms of status in employment. As a spiral, the same process represents movements through re-education and training on to higher skill levels or levels of responsibility.

Entry to full-time paid employment occurs at a later stage, generally between 18 and 23. Altogether there are seven different periods of employment; six periods of training or re-training; two periods of unemployment when a job ceases, either involuntarily (due to redundancy) or voluntarily – for home-making, child rearing, preparation for a change of direction, or for other reasons; two sabbatical periods of from six months to a year; and education other than training recurs throughout the time span. Finally, retirement from wage–earning or salaried employment to be at around 55 years of age. What the model does not show is that time spent at work is significantly less in the second model and more time can be devoted to the non-work roles identified by Donald Super and J A Bowlsbey in *Guided Career Exploration* (Psychological Corporation, New York: 1979): those of student, citizen, spouse, homemaker, leisurite, parent (and grandparent).

The past and future tenses are used with respect to the two models in order to separate them in our minds, but the reality of course is that the traditional model is still with us even if it is crumbling badly, and the emerging model is not a futuristic one. If anything, the second model tends to understate the complexity of future career patterns. In America, Europe – and even in Britain – examples of people living out this model are not hard to find. We are in a transitional phase and one of the tasks of a careers teacher is going to be bridging the old and the new for this generation of school–children.

PART 2

Careers teachers

A The role of the careers teacher

Expectations: 'As others see us'

During an in-service training course one of the HMIs was asked for a brief answer to the question, 'What do you consider to be the role of a careers teacher?' The questioner then went out onto the streets around the hotel to put the same question to the first six people he came across. Here are their answers:

Response A : '1 To broaden knowledge among pupils of work opportunities.

2 To enable pupils to become more self-assured so that 1 becomes possible.

3 To raise aspirations of pupils where possible.

4 To organise human resources to make 1, 2 and 3 possible.

5 To aid the informing of the whole curriculum with world-of-work relevance.

6 In short, to act as an informed bridge between the life in school and the life of the world-of-work, for both pupils and staff.'

(An HMI)

Response B : 'Very important! I didn't have it when I was at school. I didn't know what to do so I went off to college and trained to teach. Now I'm a hotel receptionist. I still don't know what I want to do!'

(A young woman in her mid–20s)

Response C : 'It's a jolly important one . . . but I don't really know what they actually do.'

(The mother of respondant B)

Response D : 'To try and help you to get a job. We ticked off a list, but it wasn't much help. Me dad got me this job, and it's great!'

(A local authority gardener, late teens)

Response E : To help pupils to understand what they can do, and to advise them – if they have a career in mind – whether they are likely to be capable of doing it, with or without training.'

(A bus driver)

Response F : 'To give children in their last year at school some practice at interviews, without over–training them. Above all, to give them a better idea of what a trade or job is really about. You should contact employers and employers' federations to come and talk to the pupils, and to keep you up to date on changes. I'll come and talk to your pupils if you'd like me to.'

(The owner of a hairdressing salon)

Response G : 'I don't know. Ours tried very hard to tell us about the different things we could do but in the end I didn't have much choice, did

I? Seriously though, he helped a lot of my mates and still rings up to see how I'm getting on. But there's not a lot he can do, is there?'
(An unemployed 17–year–old)

Not a very scientific survey, admittedly, but a very interesting set of responses. Try it yourself, starting with your own colleagues in school and working out into the community. You will almost certainly find the same breadth of expectation. At one extreme you'll find a comprehensive theoretical critique; at the other a total ignorance that such a role exists, or a depressing assertion that there's not a lot you can do, the economy being what it is. In between these extremes you'll find well–informed and realistic views – like those of the bus driver who must surely have been a careers teacher on industrial experience – and the views which reflect the individual needs of young people, their parents and their employers.

Now that you know what is expected of you, it will be helpful to look at the way in which careers teachers perceive their role.

'As we see ourselves'

The list which follows was drawn up by a group of experienced careers teachers. No hierarchy is intended; it is simply a list of the things which they do as careers teachers.

The role of the careers teacher is to:
– Design, implement and teach a programme of careers education
– Provide experience of the world of work
– Maintain an effective vocational and educational information service
– Offer advice and counselling
– Give option guidance
– See pupils as individuals
– Diffuse aspects of careers work into other areas of the staff/curriculum
– Involve as many staff as possible
– Liaise with external agencies, ie parents, careers officers, employers, FE, HE etc
– Maintain a record system
– Provide mock interviews
– Provide references
– Use and administer psychometric and other tests
– Build up confidence in pupils
– Help and encourage pupils
– Change the system?

These largely instrumental functions will now be placed in five groups. This should make it easier to examine the different aspects of a careers teacher's role. The groups are goal identification, careers education, careers guidance, operations management and external management.

For the sake of this analysis the following definition of a careers teacher is used as the closest to the norm: he or she is a member of staff, the bulk of whose time is assigned to careers education and guidance, and who has

the designation 'head of careers' or 'i/c careers'. Other members of staff –
usually one or two – assist with the careers education lessons.

Where the member of staff has a wider responsibility – say for the moral,
personal, vocational and life-skills development in a school – then this
analysis refers to that part of their role which is directed towards achieving the aims of careers education and guidance as defined in Part 1,
section A.

i **Goal identification**

This should include:

a Identification of the needs of the pupils in relation to careers education
and guidance: those needs which are common to them all and those
which are particular needs of individuals. Needs may occur frequently
or infrequently;
b Identification of the aims and objectives necessary to meet those needs;
c Deciding upon a list of priorities for immediate implementation.

Goal identification is probably the most neglected area in the busy
teacher's programme. Concern with achieving the limited goals set by
today's lesson, tomorrow's test, or next term's examination tends to blind
us to the underlying aims of our particular discipline and to the needs of
our pupils. Careers teachers have no such excuse. There are no examinations – other than built–in evaluation – and the relationship between the
work in hand and the ultimate aims is usually explicit rather than
implicit. In this area of education, change – as we have already seen – is
the rule rather than the exception. Consequently needs, aims and objectives have to be reviewed annually at the very least.

The process of goal identification should include all staff involved in
the education and guidance process and should be agreed with the senior
management team of the school – however narrow or wide that team
might be. Where your aims and objectives do not readily appear to be
commensurate with those of the school as a whole, you have the added
task of explaining and persuading.

ii **Careers education**

a Designing a curriculum relevant to the needs and abilities of all pupils;
b Deciding upon the necessary resources – time, space, people and materials – for implementing the curriculum;
c Choosing the appropriate methods;
d Evaluating the effectiveness of the careers education programme and
changing it where necessary.

iii **Careers guidance**

a Identifying the guidance needs of pupils;
b Identifying the place of vocational guidance within the overall pattern
of personal, academic and vocational guidance in the school;
c Designing a system of vocational guidance;

d Drawing up an annual guidance calendar;

e Deciding upon the necessary resources for implementing the guidance system;

f Evaluating the effectiveness of the guidance system and modifying it where necessary.

iv **Internal management**

This can be defined as those tasks, within the school, which are necessary in order to achieve the goals already defined.

a **Planning, organisation and co-ordination:** deciding the mechanisms which determine who does what, when, how and with whom, and seeing that it is done.

b **Staff deployment:** defining the tasks of staff with a careers education or guidance role, according to job descriptions.

c **Control of resources other than staff:** bidding for departmental funds, time and rooms. Allocating those resources efficiently, supervising the maintenance and security of rooms and materials.

d **Motivation** of your staff and pupils through personal example – especially enthusiasm and efficiency – and concern for their needs, and by means of involving them in the whole process through discussion and delegation.

e **Staff development:** seeking to provide opportunities for training, professional development and work enrichment.

f **Resolving conflict:** solving conflict between people and groups of people by negotiation, arbitration, reconciliation and use of chairmanship.

g **Communication:** ensuring that departmental channels of communication are effective and that information about the department, its aims, points of contact with, and reliance upon, other areas of the curriculum, destination of leavers etc, reaches the whole staff; and that there are effective two-way channels of communication so that feedback can be obtained and acted upon.

h **Record keeping and evaluation:** responsibility for the compilation of returns, keeping of records and registers; setting up systems, criteria and methods of evaluating the efficiency of the department in meeting the goals set.

i **Accountability:** to the headmaster/headmistress.

v **External management**

This can be defined as those tasks, performed outside the school, which are necessary in order to achieve the goals of the department. In careers, more than in any other area of the curriculum, the curriculum of the community and the world outside the school exerts a major influence on our pupils, offers a mass of resources for careers education and guidance and holds us accountable. (See B Law and A G Watts (1977) *School, Careers and Community: Church Information Office*.)

a **Parents and the community:** responsibility for informing parents and the general community of the aims and methods of the department, providing a two-way channel of communication and gaining their support and involvement in the process.

b **Employers and the community:** responsibility for two-way communication with employers, concerning their understanding of the aims and methods of the department, their expectations and employment opportunities and their role as a resource in careers education and guidance in the school and community. Responsibility for establishing similar links with all external supporting agencies: careers service, HE, FE, training organisations, CISTEL and other information bodies, trades unions, federations etc.

Teacher or manager?

Assuming that you have read the last few pages, this could well be a question you are asking. The answer of course is that all teachers are managers. The further up the ladder of responsibility, the greater the management function. Careers teachers, by virtue of their role, have more contacts to make, more channels of communication to construct, more resources to co-ordinate, than any other departmental staff.

They depend upon information from all of the departments, from group tutors/form teachers, and from heads of houses/years. They are the school's major contact with the worlds of further education, training, and employment and they have to process a mass of rapidly–changing information from these sectors. They have to be ready to respond to sudden changes in entry qualifications and dates of application, and to urgent and unpredictable requests for references.

No member of staff below deputy head status needs to be better organised than the careers teacher, *and* a better organiser. It is this fact, together with the central position of the careers teacher within the school – and between school and community – which makes the role an excellent preparation for deputy headship, and which can also alienate careers staff from colleagues unless they have established efficient channels of communication, and operate with tact and sensitivity.

Breadth of vision, good teaching ability, total commitment to careers education and guidance, the ability to build excellent relationships with young people and adults, to listen without prejudice, to develop in pupils self-reliance rather than dependence, to organise and to manage, all these are the qualities you are going to need as a careers teacher. Unless you make time to define your tasks and organise your department, the sheer weight of work will lead you into the trap of crisis management – responding from day to day to the most pressing needs – with its inevitable sense of intense pressure and frustration. Whatever you do . . . *plan ahead.*

Priorities

The analysis presented in this section has been intended to provide a detailed examination of the various roles reflected by experienced careers teachers – the majority of them with head of department status. If you are taking up a post as careers teacher for the first time it would be unreasonable to expect that you could achieve this level of organisation, especially in a school with poor existing provision. The following priorities checklist is offered as a guide towards achieving *the minimum acceptable service* and should be seen only as a starting point.

Priorities checklist
What?
The provision of sufficient vocational information, education, and guidance:

a *to enable all students to make wise decisions at each major decision-making stage* – see [D]s marked on the guidance calendar on pages 126/7 – and especially the following:
   - option choice at 14
   - alternatives at 16+, 17+, 18+

b *to enable them to make the transition to the next stage,* and especially to:
   - Employment/self-employment
   - YTS
   - Pre-vocational education
   - Further education
   - Higher education
   - Know how to occupy their time profitably – in personal terms – whilst waiting to make one of these transitions, or whilst otherwise unemployed.

Why?
Because these are the most urgent needs of our students and because these decisions and transitions tend to have important long term consequences. Options closed and transitions badly made are often difficult to reverse.

When?
a **Timing**   The appropriate points at which information, education and guidance are likely to be necessary are outlined in the guidance calendar on pages 126/7. Major decisions are marked [D].

b **Your involvement**   General vocational education and information can be provided in lessons – if they exist – during registration or tutorial time, and during year assemblies. Guidance on an individual basis could ideally take place during 'protected' non-teaching periods, but is more likely to occur during morning registration, breaktimes, lunchtimes and after school.

Who?
This will depend on the system in your school, but where provision is

scanty, you ought to rely heavily at first on:
1 yourself
2 the careers officer*
3 heads of third, fifth and sixth years (11–18 school)*
4 form tutors*
in that order, on the premise that involving more people extends the lines of communication and requires more paperwork, explaining and motivating, all of which is likely to use up precious information and guidance time which should be your first priority.

How?

If no pattern exists you will almost certainly have to begin with the 'Addition' approach – explained in the next section – for the reasons given above. It is always easier to establish a limited number of priorities and ensure that they are being met before widening the scope of your work and involving more staff. Experience will quickly dictate the division of your time between the various aspects of your work – each of which will need to be dealt with as the first priority almost on a day to day basis. References – if you are required to do them – will always have to take precedence over other administrative work, for example. Priorities include:
1 individual guidance
2 general information and education
3 administration of: references
   careers interviews for careers officer
   work experience placements
   careers library

Where?†

This will be closely prescribed by existing facilities and rooms available, but falling rolls ought to ease the situation. Suggested priorities are:
1 A 'careers room' flexible as a teaching area and vocational information area, utilising filing cabinets, box files on shelves and noticeboards inside and outside the room. If no other room is available it could be used for individual guidance outside lesson times. At least you will have a base where the students will be able to find you.
2 An interview room for careers officer interviews and for your guidance interviews. If no such room is permanently available, a suitable area should be made available for careers interviews when the careers officer is in school – not merely as a courtesy, but because the interview is so important for the students and so much more difficult in corridors, classrooms, and empty dining halls!
3 A careers library and resource area.
4 An office where records can be stored, administrative work can be done and interviews held.

*See Part 3 pages 56–63 for a detailed analysis of 2, 3 and 4.
†See 'Places' (pages 77–83) in Part 3 for a detailed examination of these areas 1–4

Conclusion These are only very limited priorities and the point has to be made that decisions are much more likely to be made wisely, and transitions smoothly – in the short run and throughout life – if there is a more comprehensive and integrated approach to careers education and guidance along the lines indicated in the next section – entitled Systems.

Systems

The devolution of responsibility for the curriculum to individual schools in England and Wales means that there are probably as many different systems as there are schools. As far as careers education and guidance is concerned, there are two basic systems which between them encompass all of the others. Tony Watts has called these basic structures the 'addition' and the 'infusion' approaches. (NICEC Training and Development Bulletin, Supplement to no 14, Spring 1980.)

i 'Addition': the careers department approach

This is by far the most common approach in schools which can be said to have a policy *and* a system of careers education and guidance.

Diagram 6 overleaf represents a fairly typical structure. It is characterised by a specialist careers department. Not uncommonly the head of department is also the sole specialist, but may draw upon other members of staff to assist with the careers education lessons. Increasingly, one of these members of staff is on permanent attachment to the department and may have some access to in–service training.

In some schools, recognition of the special role of the department in the school and community places the head of department within the senior management team – perhaps with senior teacher status. More often, the head of department is part of both the academic curriculum team *and* the pastoral development team, and is thus able to ensure that both the education and guidance aspects of the process are covered.

The advantages and disadvantages of this approach can be as follows:

Advantages
a Tasks are clear cut and well defined.
b Specialist teaching and guidance is provided by highly motivated and trained staff.
c The limited number of staff involved makes for maximum efficiency. The management tasks of communication, control, monitoring and evaluation are greatly facilitated.
d The pupils perceive careers education and guidance as an entity.

Disadvantages
a Careers education and guidance may become divorced from the rest of the curriculum – academic and pastoral.
b Viewed as just another department it may become alienated from other members of staff, especially if the head of department appears to be

Diagram 6 Careers 'addition'

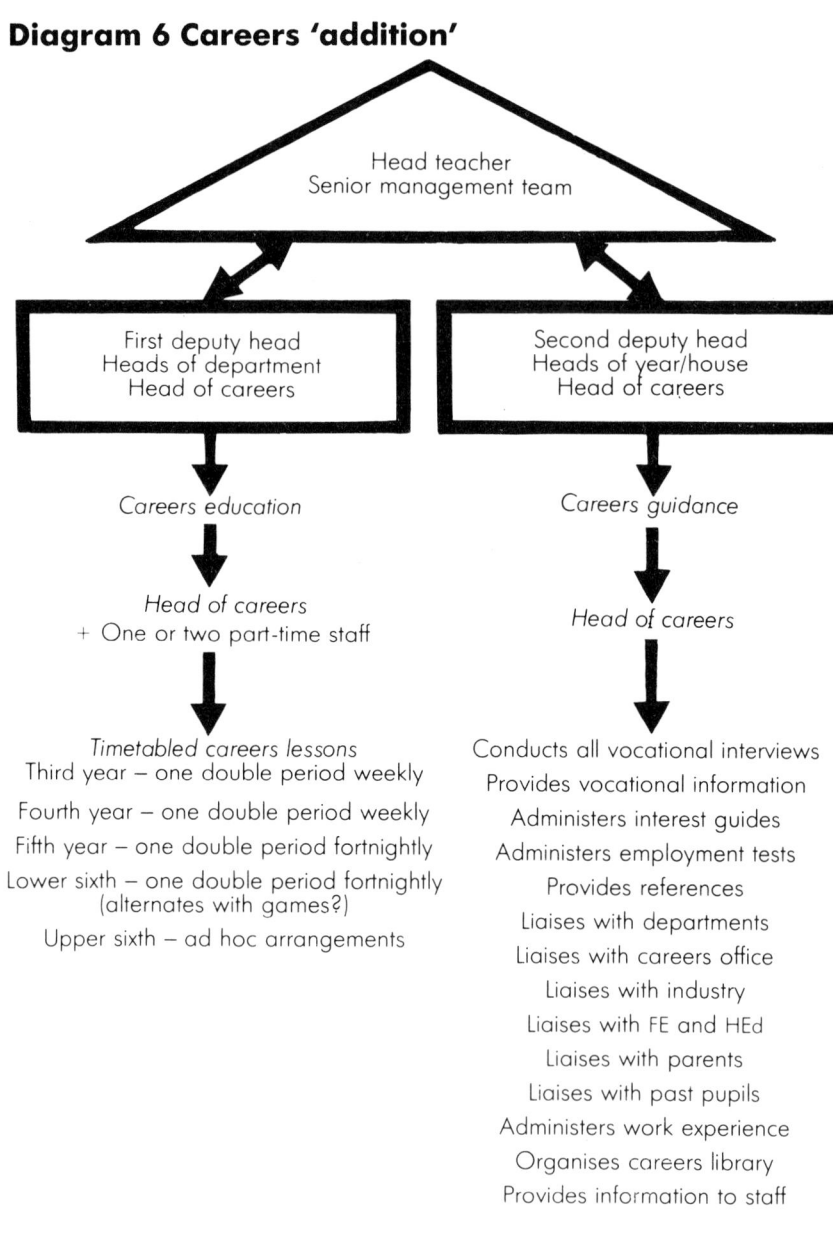

Head teacher
Senior management team

First deputy head
Heads of department
Head of careers

Second deputy head
Heads of year/house
Head of careers

Careers education

Careers guidance

Head of careers
+ One or two part-time staff

Head of careers

Timetabled careers lessons
Third year – one double period weekly

Fourth year – one double period weekly

Fifth year – one double period fortnightly

Lower sixth – one double period fortnightly
(alternates with games?)

Upper sixth – ad hoc arrangements

Conducts all vocational interviews

Provides vocational information

Administers interest guides

Administers employment tests

Provides references

Liaises with departments

Liaises with careers office

Liaises with industry

Liaises with FE and HEd

Liaises with parents

Liaises with past pupils

Administers work experience

Organises careers library

Provides information to staff

Life and social skills may appear
in the careers education programme,
or elsewhere.

The rest of the pastoral staff
concentrate on personal and
educational guidance.

straddling an academic/pastoral 'split'.

c Pupils may perceive it as just another 'subject'.

d As a relatively small department in terms of number of staff, rooms, and teaching contact time, it may be difficult to obtain the appropriate status and extra resources.

e Designated careers staff can easily be overstretched, leaving tasks unresolved. (Evaluation is always the first to go.)

ii 'Infusion': the whole curriculum approach

Less common, but gaining in popularity in response to curriculum change and falling rolls, the 'infusion' approach is represented in diagram 7 (overleaf).

Its major characteristic is the absence of a careers department as such. Careers education is dispersed throughout the curriculum and careers guidance becomes the responsibility of designated pastoral staff – usually the head of year or head of house. In this model class tutors are involved in a timetabled tutorial programme which includes elements of life and social skills work. In this sense, the pastoral network is involved in both guidance and education. Similarly, the subject departments are expected to take note of the changing vocational implications of their own disciplines and to show, as part of their teaching programme, the relevant opportunities for using the particular information and skills acquired in their subject in further education, training, employment, and the other aspects of adult life.

The central figure in this model is clearly the person who has been labelled the 'careers co-ordinator'. The complexity of the model requires a motivating, controlling and co-ordinating member of staff who has the support of the decision–making team and the respect and support of the entire staff.

The advantages and disadvantages of this approach can be as follows:

Advantages

a Careers education and guidance becomes an integral part of the curriculum, informing and giving meaning to the whole process of education.

b All staff are involved and have to be aware of the relationship between their subject and preparation for adult life.

c Careers is not perceived as merely another subject by pupils.

d Educational, personal and vocational guidance are united rather than artificially split.

e Use of resources is maximised, duplication is minimised.

Disadvantages

a The number of staff involved dramatically increases the management problem, in particular communication, organisation, monitoring and evaluation.

Diagram 7 Careers 'infusion'

Head teacher
Senior management team

Curriculum development*
Head of curriculum development
Heads of department
Careers co-ordinator
Seconded staff

Pastoral development*
Head of pastoral department
Heads of year/house
Year tutors
Careers co-ordinator

Project groups
(subject based and multi-disciplinary)

Tutorial project groups
(Development team and year tutors)

MATHS	Maths at work
	Maths for leisure
	Maths for homemaking
SCIENCE	Physical development
	Science and society
	New technologies
ENGLISH	Communication skills
	Interviewing skills
	Media studies
HOME ECONOMICS	Health
	Hygiene
	Diet
ECONOMICS	Basic economics
	The EEC/world trade
	Causes of unemployment
ART	Art at work and leisure
DESIGN TECHNOLOGY	Design for living
	Understanding industry
	Industrial links
RELIGIOUS EDUCATION	Values, ethics, morals
	Self awareness
	Relationships
MODERN LANGUAGES	European studies
	Languages at work
HISTORY	Industrial and agrarian change
	Inventions and employment
	Trades unions; the law
GEOGRAPHY	The changing world
	North and south
	Resource exploitation
LEARNING RESOURCES	Careers resources library
All depts involved in	TVEI
	Work experience
	Schools industry liaison
	Visiting speakers

HEADS OF YEAR/HOUSE
Vocational interviews
Assessments/records/reports
Careers office liaison
Work experience
References

ASSISTANT YEAR HEADS
Screening interviews
Interest guides
Collation of profiles
Responsible for group
   of year tutors

YEAR TUTORS
Timetabled tutorial
programme, includes:
 − rules and behaviour
 − relationships
 − decision making
 − choices
 − profiling
 − induction
 − learning skills

***Careers education**

***Careers guidance**

b With even a small staff turnover there needs to be a major commitment to training and motivating new staff.

c Some staff will be antipathetic or apathetic to the aims of careers education and guidance as expressed here.

d Some staff, whilst highly motivated, will lack the particular skills required of them.

e A high degree of motivation, breadth of vision, charisma, and management skills are required of the careers co-ordinator.

f There is a danger that the vocational–education part of the process can become submerged to the point where it loses its identity altogether.

g Pupils may no longer perceive the inter-relatedness of the various elements of careers education and of the processes of education and guidance.

h In the absence of good management it can be easy to get the impression that tasks are being accomplished, when in fact they are not.

Conclusions There is no such thing as an ideal system. These two models are, in any case, only models. The reality that faces you in your first appointment may be that there is no system at all. More probably there will be an approach which is closer to the 'addition' model but which uses some of the aspects of 'infusion' to spread the load and reach out into the curriculum. The purpose of this analysis has been to alert you to the fact that there are systematic approaches to careers education and guidance and that there are strengths and weaknesses inherent in each approach. If you aim to utilise the strengths and to eliminate the weaknesses, then you will succeed in achieving your aims and objectives.

PART 3

Careers education

A Designing a careers education programme

Before you start

1 Remember to start from where you are. Be aware of the constraints and of the possibilities. Always move at a pace that you and your students and colleagues can handle. Be aware of how you want the programme to develop.

2 Constantly remind yourself that for careers education *any* group of students presents a 'mixed ability' situation, in terms of interests, individual strengths/weaknesses, stage of personal and vocational development, home circumstances and so on, even if they are of similar academic ability.

3 Identify the 'continuum' of careers education from the point of entry into your school and beyond into further education, training – where it is distinct from education – employment and higher education. There is an increasing need for liaison to avoid repetition of material – as opposed to reinforcement – just as there is a danger of repetition within your own school. ('Please Miss, we did that in RE last year, English last week, and PSD yesterday!' Could easily be said of a 'self–awareness' unit, for example.)

4 Ensure that the programme complements your guidance programme in a deliberate way. Identify the decision points on your guidance calendar and let your careers lessons lead up to them.

5 Beware of trying to cover too much. All compulsory education ought to be a preparation for adult life. Your job is to isolate those elements of the curriculum which *ought to be used consciously* to meet the *particular aims* of careers education and guidance.

6 Build in some form of evaluation. Decide how you intend to discover whether specific awareness and skill objectives have been met in short term and in long term.

Objectives

At the beginning of Part 1 were quoted the aims of careers education and guidance proposed in a recent DES discussion document. If we accept those aims, then the *objectives* within the careers education programme are *intermediate goals towards achieving those aims*.

The aims themselves can be classified in the following way:
– about *self*
– about *opportunities*
– about *decisions*
– about *transitions*.
And each of these involves the development of *awareness* and *skills*.

i About self

'This above all – to thine own self be true'
William Shakespeare

Clearly, one cannot become self–directing unless one knows oneself. The terms usually applied to this process are 'self–concept' or 'self-awareness'. One of the major struggles of adolescence is the gradual emergence of the self–directing individual, whilst still retaining essential ties with family and peer groups. It is this individual who is going to have to choose between alternative routes and goals and to decide on priorities where a number of goals might clash – 'student/spouse/worker', for example. To do this, that individual ought to be able to answer the questions:

'What is the full range of my abilities?' (ie capability)
'What is the full range of my interests?' (ie interests)
'What is the range of my needs?' (ie needs)
'What is the range of my values?' (ie values)

There are two important points here. Firstly, the use of the phrase 'full range' is to emphasise that only by knowing the full extent of one's abilities, interests, needs and values – from high to low – can one know the *range of occupations* which one is likely to be *capable of*, likely to be *motivated to* and likely to be *satisfied by*.

Secondly, all of these categories are subject to change through life. Improved competency, acquiring of new skills, new interests, changing needs and shifting values, is the essence of human development. Self-–concept is therefore a shifting concept, and self–awareness is an ongoing process. This means that self–analysis, in the sense implied here, ought to occur regularly throughout the careers programme and is essential to the guidance process.

Any information about oneself which is clearly understood and assimilated and can be used to answer the questions posed above, will be an *awareness* objective. Any skills which are learnt in the process of gaining such information, and can be used by the student for the same purpose in the future, will meet a *skills* objective. Such skills will include knowing what questions to ask of oneself, being able to identify and eliminate self–bias, being able to use other people to test your own answers, being able to use tests, grids, and other aids.

In the context of careers education, self–awareness is only helpful when it can be related by the student to the opportunities available.

ii About opportunities

How do adults use their talents, and occupy their time
a in order to accumulate income for material goods and services?
b in order to satisfy their other needs?
Which of these occupations are open to me?
What will they *really* be like?

47

What do I have to do in order to embark on them?

All young people – before they make the transition from compulsory education to the next stage – ought to be able to answer these questions and know how and where to find increasingly sophisticated answers. This is commonly known as developing the *occupational concept*.

The term 'occupational concept' is normally related to awareness of employment opportunities, and the term *extra–occupational concept* is used for activities outside of paid employment. In view of the changing patterns of opportunity examined in Part 1, occupational concept is the term used to cover all possible occupations, paid or otherwise.

How far will *my* needs be met by different occupations, and by different combinations of occupation?

Young people can only begin to make informed decisions about their future when they are able to relate their understanding of occupations to their understanding of their own needs. This matching of self–awareness and opportunity awareness is normally called the occupational self-concept.

iii **About decisions**

How do I decide which alternative to choose?

Whether the alternatives being considered are the options at 13 +, at the end of compulsory schooling, or beyond, our pupils need a strategy to help them to decide.

The skills involved in assessing their own abilities, interests and values, the alternatives open to them, the reliability of their sources of information, the advantages and disadvantages of the various alternatives, the implications of their final choice and in the provision of a backup or contingency plan in the event of being disappointed, are considerable. Unless they learn how to choose for themselves – and the role of guidance in the process – then they will never become self–directing and will always have someone else to blame for unsatisfactory decisions.

The awareness of decision–making as a strategy which they can control and the acquisition of deciding skills come under the heading *decision making*. The dramatic growth of helping agencies over the last three decades reflects the absence of these skills in a world which is becoming increasingly complex, and which requires greater flexibility and more frequent decisions. Once gained, these skills are surely skills for life.

iv **About transition**

One of the primary aims of careers education has always been to prepare young people for the next stage of their lives following the end of compulsory education. Often this has been limited – by time and resources – to helping them to decide where to go next. Increasingly schools are beginning to recognise that it is also their responsibility to help them to make that transition as smoothly as possible.

Having chosen a course of action the two questions which our students

will want us to help them to answer are:
- How do I apply?
- How can I maximise my chance of being accepted?

The skills involved here will involve all of those we have already considered, plus the specific skills involved in using letters of application, curriculum vitae, application forms, interviews and preliminary visits to the full. The skills involved are usually classed as *communication skills*, but it is important to remember that these are only one particular application of this branch of skills which spans the whole of the learning process and will occur frequently throughout the careers programme.

The other sort of questions which we ought to be helping our students to answer include:
- What will I need when I start training/FE/HE/seeking employment?
- Where can I get what I need?
- Whom do I have to contact?
- Whom ought I to contact?
- What will it be like?
- What will be expected of me in terms of behaviour and attitude?
- What can I do to help myself to settle in quickly?

Essentially, these questions require awareness and skills which can be classified under the headings 'information' and 'coping'. The areas which we might expect to cover will include:
- sources of information and help
- accommodation – living at home; living away from home
- finance and budgeting
- other learning environments
- study skills
- leisure environments
- changing relationships
- new relationships
- unemployment – coping, and using your time productively.

NB Unemployment figures in this list, using the definition of employment as criterion – ie an occupation which is rewarded by money or other material payments. But by definition then FE and training would be included under the term unemployment. In any case, many 'unemployed' people do occupy their time in ways which are materially rewarded.

It would be most productive therefore to examine the ways in which people who are not occupied in employment, education and training spend their time, and to consider how they might finance themselves, budget, use their leisure time and seek new alternatives. There is no need to labour the term, unemployment, with all of its connotations; far better to examine *all* of the alternatives when dealing with each of the topics listed. Individual needs will be met by specific guidance from yourself or the careers office and other helping agencies. Aim to be positive, and encourage your students to be.

Fortunately an increasing number of institutions – of employment and of education – include an induction course as part of their introduction to new recruits and this element of the course will therefore tend to be a matter of liaison and partnership between school, FE, HE, employment and training agencies. The trap to avoid is the assumption that it can safely be left to someone else to make provision for a smooth transition.

Summary

These objectives seek to help young people to become self–directing; to make the first of many decisions about the kind of life they would like to lead; to make the first transition towards adult life as smoothly and successfully as possible. Because the process is going to continue throughout their lives, we hope that the awareness and the skills which they begin to develop through these objectives will help them to live a full, productive and more satisfying life. It is likely that they will begin to learn these skills earlier in their lives, but like any skill they will need to be reinforced until they become as comfortable to use as the alphabet or the multiplication table.

Diagram 8 (below) attempts to describe the sequence involved in the growth of occupational maturity. The process is by no means as straightforward as the model suggests and it continues throughout life, but hopefully it serves to reinforce the points made in this chapter.

Diagram 8 The process of vocational maturation

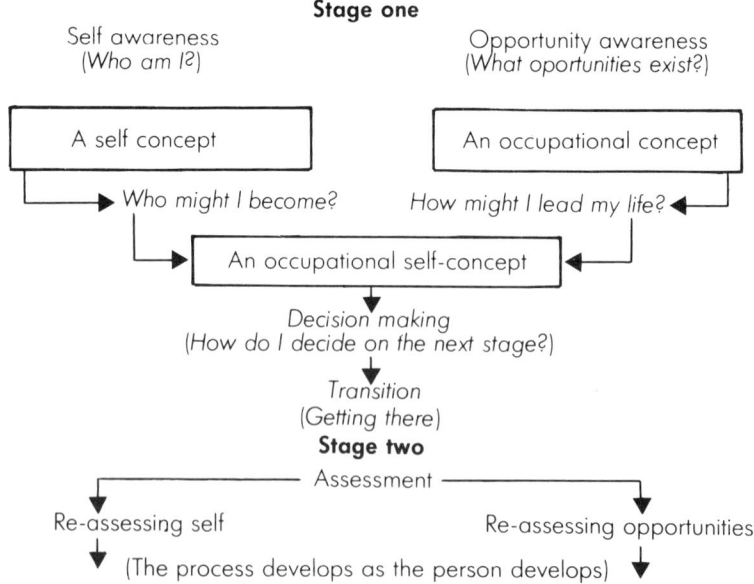

B Methods

Definition : The learning procedure; the *manner* in which learning strategies are presented. Not to be confused with the people, place, and things, which make up the learning *resources.*

The methods used as part of a careers education programme will be those which are available to the rest of the curriculum. The unique role of careers education both requires and enables a wider range of learning strategies to be used than that which is characteristic of other school–based subjects.

Because careers education seeks to relate students' experiences and skills to the world outside the school and to adult life beyond it, it follows that the methods should use experience wherever possible to reinforce learning. Learning through doing, feeling, and expressing is still too much of a rarity outside the practical and aesthetic areas of the curriculum. There are ample reasons why this is so, but none of them excuse its absence from the careers education programme.

Diagram 9 (below) presents the range of methods commonly used in teaching programmes, along a continuum from abstract/theoretical at the top, to concrete/experiential at the bottom. We can examine the strengths and limitations of each in turn.

Diagram 9 Methods: from theory to direct experience

Abstract/theoretical	lecture
	talk
	discussion
increasingly	exercise/programmed learning
	projects
	skill instruction
	role play
	case study
	work experience
Concrete/experiential	direct experience

A lecture

Definition: An informative talk which makes little if any allowance for participation on the part of the students, other than listening, note–taking and questions on points of clarification.

Advantages: Where resources are limited – time, space, availability of speakers – and where the information is intended for a large group of students, precise information can be provided without the distraction of discussion.

Disadvantages: The lack of participation by the students will shorten their threshold of boredom, and limit assimilation of information – especially when the subject matter is sequential, describing a decision–making strategy for example. These disadvantages can be overcome by using a number of speakers, a variety of visual/audio aids, by encouraging notemaking and by making it clear from the outset that time will be provided at the end for points arising from the lecture on an informal basis.

A talk

Definition: An informative talk, with a smaller group of students, which allows for participation on the part of the students in the form of questions, answers and comment.

Advantages: The limited size of the group – ideally less than 20 – and the involvement of the students aids concentration and interest whilst retaining a specific theme.

Disadvantages: Over–participation on the part of a few students can 'switch off' the others in the group. Irrelevant questions and misdirected comment can divert attention from the theme. Under–participation can reduce the talk to an apologetic monologue.

A discussion

Definition: An open exchange of information, ideas or opinions, on an agreed topic among a small group which may consist entirely of students or include the teacher and adults other than teachers.

Advantages: It can encourage greater concentration, interest and communication by showing that the students' opinions and experiences are valued. Where adults other than teachers are equal partners in the discussion it can also remove the barriers between 'adult/teacher' and 'student' which restrict understanding and freedom of expression on both sides. Students become more open to ideas and to contradictory points of view when their own opinions are valued.

Disadvantages: In the absence of agreed rules and procedures and well–defined tasks, the discussion can be diverted from the theme, take the form of an argument, entrench students in their views, and exclude some of the students altogether.

NB Whenever you wish to encourage students to offer information, ideas, or opinions, the following method reduces the fear of ridicule or dismissal and encourages every student to participate:

a *The individual brainstorm* Students are given a specific point to consider and asked to write down any facts, ideas or opinions which they think might be relevant, without according them a priority or worrying about their validity.

b *Pyramiding* They are then asked to share their list with a partner and between them arrive at a joint list. All of the paired lists are then shared within a larger group to arrive at a group list. One member of the group is then deputed to describe the group list to the whole class, with clarification from his own group when required. The relative anonymity of the procedure, the notion of sharing and the controlled examination of ideas within a fairly strict timescale all help to make participation and discussion effective. This is particularly important in a careers programme where we are dealing with personal ideas, interests and values, and are aiming to help our students to become self–directing.

An exercise
Definition: A set task of relatively short duration which is usually intended to reinforce or test assimilation of skills or knowledge. When the exercise is highly structured and presented on a computer or similar teaching machine, it is called *programmed learning*. Exercises and computer programmes are becoming increasingly common in careers education and there is a lot of scope for teachers and students to design their own.

Advantages: The students are involved – either individually or in groups – in an *active* process of problem–solving. The structure of the exercise ensures that the desired sequence of learning takes place and that the students are aware of any gaps in their understanding.

Disadvantages: Used too often, without adequate explanation or follow–up, they may be regarded by students as time–fillers or mere tests.

A project
Definition: A task – similar to an extended exercise – which requires the student to decide which methods and resources to use in order to complete the task.

Advantages: The student has the opportunity to become personally involved – individually or as part of a team – in a thorough examination of a particular topic or problem. There is ample opportunity for the development of information skills, initiative and creativity. Provided that the student is able to choose/negotiate the nature of the project it is likely to foster interest, perseverance, pride in work and self–confidence. An example of such a project would be research into a job family closest to a student's interests, abilities and aspirations.

Disadvantages: In view of the commitment expected for a project and the amount of time spent on one, it is essential that the student sees the relevance of the project to his needs. All of the ingredients for successful completion of the task should be built into it for each student. Continual guidance will have to be a feature of project work for most students in order to build up confidence and the skills of gathering, interpreting and using information.

A skill instruction
Definition: A session during which a specific skill is *explained* and *demonstrated* to students who then have the opportunity to *practise* it for themselves.

Advantages: It is possible to present the skill to a group of students. The skill can be broken down into its component parts and learnt in manageable stages, provided that this is the most appropriate method. Examples in careers education would include JIIG-CAL; using interest guides; using the careers library/Signposts; completing a curriculum vitae; preparing for interviews; etc.

Disadvantages: None. Beware of leaving too little time for practice; of breaking a skill down too far; of attempting to instruct too large a group with too few resources – eg demonstrating Signposts to 30 students with only one pack of Signposts.

A game
Definition: A contrived situation – usually removed from real life settings but reflecting aspects of the work place or human behaviour – which introduces elements of skill, competition and chance. The intention is to use students' natural enjoyment of games to enable them to appreciate aspects of life and work, through emotional involvement or empathy. Always followed by a discussion/debriefing.

Advantages: Students tend to enjoy and enter wholeheartedly into these games and they can provide powerful learning experiences.

Disadvantages: Some students will refuse to become involved or may deliberately disrupt the game. Some will cheat – but this is a feature of life outside of games and can be used in the debriefing. Because the games are not 'real' there is a strong possibility that many of the students will not be able to relate their experiences during the game with outside experiences. Many of us behave in games in ways in which we would never dream of doing outside them. The enjoyable or distressing experiences of the game will tend to dominate, rather than the intellectual points made in the de–briefing. The rules of the game must be rigidly imposed and the objectives limited. Staff using them should be comfortable and confident in operating them. Despite this list of cautions find out about careers games and discover how best to use them. They are useful and prove that learning can be fun.

A role play
Definition: Students are asked to adopt a role within a given situation and to behave in a manner appropriate to their understanding of that role. Usually the situation is one which involves practice of problem solving, decision making or communication skills.

Advantages: An excellent way of providing an opportunity for students to practise and appreciate the roles which they may enter when they leave school or which may confront them through other people. It enables students to explore and analyse behaviour and attitudes and their consequences, in a controlled and protected setting.

Disadvantages: Care must be taken to involve students who lack confidence or who are easily embarrassed in a manner which will build up rather than lessen their confidence. Requiring them to 'perform' for their fellow students is likely to be counterproductive. Work in pairs or small groups over a period of time will help to overcome this problem.

A case study

Definition: The presentation of a situation – preferably real – which the students are required to study. They are then expected either to diagnose the particular problem, or suggest a possible solution, or both.

Advantages: It is possible to provide the students with real life situations which they may meet and give them the chance to use the skills which will be demanded of them. It should help them to understand a little better what it will really be like in similar situations. The fact that many of the case studies are based on fact adds a serious element to the exercise which often produces a high degree of concentration and motivation.

Disadvantages: An isolated case study – however factual – cannot duplicate the actual experience of diagnosing or solving a problem under 'real' conditions. Where possible, the constraints which exist outside the classroom – especially time – should be introduced gradually into the case studies to simulate conditions as closely as possible.

NB Students should also be encouraged to observe similar situations during periods of work experience, compare them with the case studies they have taken part in and devise their own for use by the class.

Work experience: occupational experience

Definition: Structured experience, on a short time basis, of work, voluntary work, or challenging leisure pursuits.

Advantages: A detailed examination of work and occupational experience as a resource appears in the next section. As a method, it offers the learning situation closest to a full–time occupation. There is no substitute for 'first hand' experience, and on return to the classroom there is time for reflection and analysis and a sharing of experiences.

Disadvantages: In order for the experience to be both valid and useful a lot of preparation, monitoring and follow up should take place. In the absence of effective planning students can come to view this as a job–tasting session – which it is not – valuable observation time can be wasted and colleagues will argue that the benefits of such experience do not compensate for 'lessons' missed.

Direct experience

Definition: Regular experience of work, voluntary work, or leisure pursuits, during which the students are able to participate as fully as possible, using the identical skills and experiencing the same things as non–students. Although provision tends to be limited for this method within school time there are possibilities: remedial reading and adult literacy schemes, voluntary work and community service, for example. Many of our students have part-time jobs and regular hobbies and leisure pursuits. These are valuable experiences which ought to be consciously related to relevant parts of the careers programme.

Preparing for interviews

An example using a topic to show how the different methods can be used.

A lecture   A lecture by a personnel officer to a large group of students, on the purpose and nature of interviews and how best to prepare for one.

A talk   A talk entitled 'Be prepared' to small groups of students, by a personnel officer or admissions tutor, using slides or a short film and encouraging questions.

A discussion   Small groups of students – each with an employer – to discuss 'How to prepare', 'Do's and don'ts', and 'Handling the interview'.

An exercise   Students to complete a *personal checklist* in preparation for an interview to which they might reasonably be called in the near future – YTS; employment; FE; HE.

A project   Pairs of students to research a specific job using *Signposts* and the *SPEEDCOP* classification; to draw up a relevant interview record form for a potential interviewer covering all of the relevant aspects and with a graded assessment system; to explain the form to the other pairs of students.

A skill instruction   Demonstration and practice of dress, deportment, eye to eye contact, manner etc. Possible use of video camera for self–analysis.

A game   A simulation of 'outrageous' interviews, using the *New Faces* style of assessment of marks for presentation, content, and star quality.

A role play   Students take on the roles of interviewers and interviewees, prepare for role play, and de–brief each other on 'serious' interviews. Increasingly, schools are able to persuade local employers/members of Rotary or the Soroptimists to take on the role of interviewer and to join in the de–briefing.

A case study   1 Local firms are often happy to provide examples of job specifications and to explain problems which they have in finding suitable applicants. This information can be used to create case studies requiring students to diagnose or to suggest solutions to the problem. 2 Schools' television and video programmes provide excellent examples of filmed interviews which can be used as case studies in the same way.

Work experience   Interviews ought to be part of a work experience induction, and would have the added bonus of ensuring that students are prepared for periods of work experience.

Direct experience   Many students are interviewed for part–time jobs or are called for interview before they leave school. If they are shown how to use de–briefing forms they can learn consciously from the experience and help other students at the same time by feeding into a reservoir of information on methods and styles of interviewing.

NB None of these methods taken in isolation would form an adequate preparation for interviews. As always, the art of teaching is to select the appropriate combination of methods and resources and the best order in which to present them for a particular group of students. Clearly, there is no excuse for a 'chalk and talk' approach to careers education as far as methods are concerned, and the section which follows examines the practical use of a wide range of resources.

C Resources

Definition : The *people, places* and *things* used in learning strategies. The range of resources available for careers education is wider than for any other subject area, if only because careers education is concerned with all of the occupational aspects of adult life. As with methods, the problems are those of identification, selection and use of resources. The more resources you intend to use, the greater the organisational skills you will have to acquire, but the more effective and satisfying your work will become.

The purpose of this section is to examine the range of resources commonly used in careers education programmes and to indicate briefly how they may be used.

There are three resources in particular which have been singled out for more detailed examination because they have a major role to play. They are the careers officer, the careers library and work experience.

i People

Inasmuch as everybody represents a particular lifestyle and occupational pattern, then everyone is a potential resource for a careers education programme. Well–documented research has shown that people outside of school exert a dominant influence – often *the* dominant influence – on the formation of occupational self–concepts. This is hardly surprising, since there are far more role–models in the community than in the school and it would be surprising if parents especially were not influential in affecting the future of their children.

Unfortunately, people – and that includes teachers – can be well–intentioned sources of misinformation when occupational and employment conditions are subject to such rapid change. Rather than trying to ignore or counteract such influences one of your tasks is to harness them, in order to strengthen your education and guidance programmes. By bringing the community into the school and taking the school into the community, you can show your students how to learn critically from the influences to which they are already subject, show the school how to use the community as a curricular resource and hopefully inform the community of the work which the school is attempting, and their role within it. Essentially, you should be trying to create the 'informed bridge' referred to by the HMI when defining the careers teacher's role.

Despite the rigours of the current economic climate your first surprise will be how willing people are to give up their time to help pupils. Some – like the banks and voluntary agencies – will often approach you for permission to come into school; others will readily respond to invitations.

Your major problem ought to be finding the time to accommodate the number of people willing and able to enrich your programme.

Diagram 10 (below) provides a guide to the range of resources in this category. Some of the distinctions are necessarily arbitrary. Careers officers are usually designated to one or more schools and are based in schools for much of their time, but strictly speaking they are external to official school staffing. Some of the other specialists have a dual role similar to that of the careers officer in that they are both providers of guidance – and information for guidance – as well as participants in the careers education programme. All of the groups listed as 'other resources' are specialists in their own roles. Nevertheless, it is worth defining your resources in this way to see if you are relying too much on one area and neglecting valuable sources of information, stimulus and skill provision in others.

Before examining the potential of each of these groups it may help to bear in mind this checklist of points to consider when using people as a resource.

Diagram 10

Ci **People**

Internal (school-based)   **External** (community-based)

i(a) **Careers specialists**

Careers teachers   Careers officers

i(b) **Other specialists**

Subject teachers   Schools industry liaison officers
                                                             Project Trident co-ordinators
Guidance staff   Specialised agencies:
                                                             (Educational welfare,
Head/deputies   educational psychologists,
                                                             health services, youth services,
                                                             voluntary agencies, churches,
                                                             FEd, HEd, CISTEL, Civil, Social
                                                             and Public services)

Pupils   i(c) **Other resources**   Employers
Ancillary staff   employees   ⎧ as parents
                                                                                ⎪ students
                                                             Past pupils   ⎨ YTS
                                                                                ⎪ Vol workers
                                                             Parents   ⎪ Employees
                                                                                ⎩ Claimants

                                                             Trade unions

                                                             Round table/Soroptimists

                                                             Sports Council

                                                             Leisure centres

a Explore the potential of this person or group of people in relation to your objectives.

b Decide how, and for what purpose, you would like to use this person.

c Find out how this person is expecting to be used and for what purpose.

d Negotiate a satisfactory agreement on the part that this person will play in your programme. It may be that a potential resource will have as his main aim a public relations exercise, or appeal, on behalf of his company, service or voluntary organisation. If that is not appropriate within the context of your programme it may be possible to provide an opportunity for such an appeal in an assembly or another part of the curriculum. Be prepared to offer such alternative quid pro quos but equally be prepared to say no to well-meant offers if they are inappropriate, and to explain why.

e Brief visitors fully in terms of the *objective* and its place in the overall programme, the *number* of students, their *age* and range of *intellectual ability*, the *time* available, the *room* to be used and *other resources* available.

f Check that you are able to provide audio–visual resources requested, and have met all of the other needs outlined.

g Offer to arrange a preliminary visit so that the visitor can familiarise himself with the school, the arrangements and perhaps even the group of students. For all but the most experienced visitors, schools present a considerable challenge to their nerves and confidence – something which teachers themselves take some time to overcome but are surprisingly quick to forget.

h Confirm the time and date in writing and check the day before that everything is in order.

i Brief and prepare the students for the visit, exploring the sort of points which they ought to be considering and the kind of questions which they might wish to ask. Do not provide them with a list of questions or put questions into their minds; discuss the topic and let them formulate their own questions. Beware of covering ground which the visitor will be introducing.

j Inform your colleagues through the normal channels – staff bulletin or noticeboard – and introduce your visitor to some of your colleagues. There is something particularly chilling about being the 'stranger in the staffroom'. Apart from the courtesy involved, it may well be that other members of staff would welcome the opportunity to involve your visitor in some of their work, or would be prepared to provide a service to your visitor.

k Meet, welcome, refresh, and thank your visitor, on the day in question.

l Discuss the outcome. Both of you will be certain to learn something during a de-briefing session. Be sure to tell your visitor how you think the session went, and how the students felt about it. Invariably, visitors think that silence and lack of obvious response equates with boredom, when it can often mean that young people are thinking, and reflecting.

m Discuss possible ways of following up the session, and arrangements for future involvements. Thank your visitor again, in writing or by telephone.

If all of this seems to be rather formal, remember that you are initially concerned with building up contacts and exploring ways in which people can assist you with your programme. As some of your visitors begin to become regulars and are instantly recognised as friends of the school in the staffroom and by the students, so your arrangements will become more relaxed and instinctive. But there is then the danger that your programme may become stale and repetitive. Do not let this happen, and do not rely too much on a narrow selection of tried and trusted people.

i(a) **The careers specialists**

Careers officers

There is one organisation which was set up with the express role of acting as a bridge between school and work, both for you and for your students – your LEA careers service. For over 70 years such a service has been available to young people. The Juvenile Employment Service and its successor the Youth Employment Service assisted young people under the age of 18 or still at school. In 1973 the Employment and Training Act abolished the age limit and imposed on all LEAs the duty to provide a vocational guidance service for people attending educational institutions and an employment service for people leaving them. In most areas this service continues automatically up to two years after completion of full–time education and often is made available to graduates seeking initial advice. The main functions of the careers service as outlined by the Department of Employment in 1976 were:

'– to work with careers and guidance teachers in schools and colleges in the careers education of young people, and to provide them and their parents with information on educational, employment and training opportunities;

– to give continuing vocational guidance to pupils and students in their later years at school or college, and to help them reach informed and realistic decisions about their careers;

– to help young people to find suitable training and employment and employers to find suitable workers; and

– to offer help and advice to young people on problems connected with their settlement in employment.' DOE PL 585

How far these functions have been carried out – and are being carried out at this moment – depends on a number of factors. There is no careers service as such, but rather a number of careers services. Each LEA has autonomy over its own service and operates under guidelines from the Department of Employment. Not only is there much variety between different LEAs, but it also exists between individual careers officers within their own services. If you are going to be able to enjoy a fruitful relationship with your careers service then it is important that you understand the dichotomy which exists within the service at present.

There are two basic philosophies applied to the work of a careers officer, and a multitude of combinations. On the one hand there are those who believe that the emphasis should be upon the functions related to the provision of *information, pre–selection*, and *placement*, with the availability of other services determined by the amount of manpower, time and other resources remaining. On the other hand there are those who believe that the *education* and *vocational guidance* functions are paramount in determining realistic placement and should be available to all.

Cuts in local government spending have sharpened the debate, and with the expansion of the YTS there is increased pressure on careers officers to assist with pre–selection and placement. The future role, organisation and control of the service is currently under review by the government. If control does move from the LEAs to the MSC then it may be that the information, pre–selection, and placement role will become virtually exclusive and this will necessarily affect the relationship between careers teachers and careers officers.

The existence of these two philosophies also helps to explain the antipathy of some schools, and their hierarchies in particular, to careers officers. Some resent the intrusion of what they see as a 'placement officer' guiding their able pupils away from the sixth form. Some schools expect the careers officers to teach their careers programme for them, others resent any involvement in what is a 'teaching' role.

These scenarios are less common than they used to be but ought not to exist at all. If they exist in your school it will be because there is no accepted careers philosophy in the school, or because of some unfortunate past experiences. If you want to make optimum use of your careers service then you have to know what it can provide, what it is prepared to provide and arrive at a close working relationship with careers officers attached to your school. They may well become your best professional friends and strongest allies.

What they can provide

In a careers office you are likely to find the following:

Specialists dealing with particular guidance or placement needs. A *disablement officer* to assist handicapped students and to advise their schools; an *unemployment officer* who may concentrate upon long–term unemployed persons and set up appropriate schemes; a number of *YTS liaison officers* to assist with guidance and placement on appropriate training schemes; an *industrial liaison officer*, an *older leaver* specialist and so on.

Teams of careers officers attached to schools and colleges and offering all, or most, of the following services:

Information for students, parents and teachers regarding different occupations: employment, training, further and higher education and voluntary work. Such information includes entry requirements, the nature of the occupation, the opportunities which the occupations present.

At the appropriate time information is given regarding the *school leaving procedure*, including registration at the careers office, eligibility for claiming benefit, acquisition of national insurance number, taxation in employment, and arrangements for YTS, placement, and guidance interviews when compulsory education has ceased.

The Educational Counselling and Credit Transfer Information Service (ECCTIS), designed by the Open University, is available at careers offices. It enables students either to discover courses which are open to them in FE and HE *before* they leave the sixth form or to transfer from one higher level course to another with greater ease during the first or subsequent years at university, polytechnic or college. This computerised information service will also be of great benefit to potential mature students.

Following the publication of A–level results, the *Further Education Information Service* (FEIS) is available at the careers office. Computer lists of polytechnic, college and institute courses undersubscribed are discussed with students who are as yet unplaced and information and guidance are offered in relation to courses, the university clearing system and other alternatives.

Education   Many careers officers will assist with the *design* of a careers education programme. By virtue of their wide contacts with schools within the LEA and with other authorities they will certainly be able to *arrange a contact* with other schools which have well–established programmes and who would be happy to discuss them with you.

Most careers offices have a wide variety of *software resources* for careers education and operate a loan service. Games, case studies and simulations, videos, film strips and tapes are often available. In most areas the *careers service operates as a bulk purchaser of CRAC, COIC and other material on behalf of schools*, thus saving a considerable discount for schools.

All attached careers officers will *meet groups* of students as part of a school's careers programme. Some will be willing and able to become involved in sessions in which they have a special expertise – role play, interview techniques, case studies etc – while many will *operate the JIIG-CAL and JKI* presentations which require special training.

Guidance   *Individual interviews* with students in their final year at school, and when requested at other times, are the most easily identifiable aspects of a careers officer's work in school. There is considerable controversy surrounding the appropriate clientele for these interviews. Whether or not there should be 'blanket' interviews of all students, interviews of 'selected' students on the recommendation of careers teachers, or by 'self–selection', depends upon the prevailing philosophy in the school and in the careers service.

Whatever system is agreed it is certainly desirable that all students should be interviewed by a careers teacher before seeing the careers officer, that notes are made available to both parties, and difficult cases discussed before and after interview sessions.

Parents may be invited to attend the careers interview, and again there are arguments for and against. Ideally, a full explanation of the careers and guidance programme, and the purpose of the careers interview, should be given to parents. In well–organised schools it is not uncommon for parents to become better informed than their sons and daughters and yet less directive than would otherwise have been the case.

Guidance interviews continue to be available to unemployed young people, older leavers and any young people considering changing their employment or course of training/education. In some areas this service is available to older people and in this way the careers office is able to monitor the overall effectiveness of its work from school to early adulthood.

In addition to the fifth year interview, and equivalent interviews in sixth forms and colleges, individual interviews are given by request of the student and will include information–giving, occupational interest guides and tests, CASCAID (see page 100) sessions, and assistance with decision–making.

Placement The intention of all non–directive guidance – no, this isn't a contradiction in terms – is that the client should be able to place himself/herself. The placement role of the careers officer is usually concerned with providing information about employment, training and educational opportunities for the student, and limited information about the student for the employer. Whilst this may involve the careers officer in the arrangement of interviews and some degree of pre–selection, the onus is on the interviewee to make the most of the opportunity to 'sell' himself and to find out about the firm/college, and for the employer to 'sell' the firm and to find out if the applicant is suitable for the post. Hopefully, both of the participants are going to be honest in their projections and the careers officer will only ever be an honest and professional broker with the welfare of the student paramount.

Liaison To the extent that the careers office provides information to schools about industry, commerce and the service sector, higher and further education and about secondary education to those sectors, it is well placed to encourage liaison between them. Although this is not one of the declared aims of the careers service, many careers officers pass on information about open days, visits and visiting speakers, and assist with the planning of school and LEA careers conventions. In some authorities the careers service co-ordinates Project Trident (see page 67), work experience schemes, schools and industry liaison and teacher industrial placements.

Training In recent years the training of careers officers has become increasingly professional, and regular in–service courses are available after initial qualification. This has resulted in a greater involvement of the careers service in joint careers teacher/careers officer workshops, joint attendance at LEA in–service courses and CRAC/NICEC training modules, and the setting up of local training consortia with careers teachers and officers among the trainers as well as the trainees. The resulting interchange of experience and ideas is proving beneficial to all concerned and is particularly valuable in the development of common philosophies and better awareness of complementary roles.

How you can help your careers officer

a Ensure that your careers officer is fully conversant with the philosophy, curriculum and organisational systems within the school.

b Discuss your careers programme and guidance calendar, and agree appropriate points of intervention and firm dates.

c Ensure that the normal courtesies are shown whenever your careers officer is in school, and that adequate rooms are provided for individual interviews – even if it means fighting for internal building alterations to convert unused space into an interview room.

d Explain the purpose of the careers interview to your colleagues and the use to which any of the information they are being asked to provide will be put. Only if they receive relevant and comprehensive information about the pupils they are interviewing can the careers officers be expected to achieve anything substantial in a half–hour interview.

e Make sure that you are fully conversant with the philosophy, personnel and systems within your careers office.

f Make sure that your students understand the role which the careers officers can play and the limits to their services, and that the students are well prepared for their interview.

g To the extent that his or her time will allow, see to it that your careers officer becomes a familiar and welcome figure in the staffroom, in teaching groups and at parents' evenings.

In these ways you will also be helping your students to derive the maximum benefit from the careers service, not just while they are at school, but for some time afterwards.

i(b) **Other specialists:**

Subject teachers

Subject teachers can be a resource for careers education and guidance in a number of ways. In a school which has adopted the 'infusion' approach, subject teachers will be expected to relate parts of their subject curriculum directly to careers; some teachers in other schools will see this as part of their duty regardless of whether or not it is laid down in the syllabus. Many subject teachers have personal or secondhand knowledge of employment, training, and especially higher education opportunities related to their subject, and may pass this information on either in an organised or an accidental manner.

Given that all of this takes place, one of your responsibilities is to see that all teachers in your school understand the careers philosophy and system, and how they can best contribute to it. If they are going to be a source of information, then you have a part to play in providing them with up–to–date information about the vocational implications of their subjects. It may be the responsibility of the heads of department – persuade them that it is – but you are in an ideal position to pass on relevant information about changing requirements, courses and employment structures, to encourage them to accompany groups on industrial and educational visits and to take up industrial placements themselves under LEA schemes.

Arrange for careers officers, industrialists and other employers to talk to the staff about new schemes and changing employment patterns. Only in this way is it likely that internal curriculum change will be relevant to the needs of our students after they have left us.

If you want to enlist the support of your colleagues as a positive resource, then it must involve you initially in a considerable amount of information–giving, and the development of planned involvement by staff, in your work.

Guidance staff

Vocational guidance is impossible in isolation, which means that you have to rely upon and assist other members of the pastoral system in your school, especially from the end of the second secondary year upwards.

You are going to need a total profile of the students' academic, personal, medical and social characteristics and history – up to date, and in a form which can be helpful to the careers officer as well as to yourself, but above all which is understood by the student.

Regardless of whether or not they are involved in teaching or co-ordinating a personal development, life, or social skills programme, the guidance staff will be gaining information and affecting a student's development of self–awareness, decision making and coping skills each time they interview him.

Everything which has been suggested about subject staff is equally true for guidance staff and if you hope to, or have to, use group tutors and heads of year or house in careers guidance as outlined in the 'infusion' approach, then you will have a major in–service exercise to initiate, as opposed to a minor one.

Heads and deputies

These personnel are often well informed about curriculum change and frequently have the opportunity to visit places of employment and of higher education. Because of their major influence over curriculum and resources, you have to be sure that they are conversant with your teaching and guidance programmes. Encourage them to help you to make useful contacts in the community, to develop staff and parental co-operation and to take an active interest in your work. Whether it is wise to involve them in regular careers teaching is another matter. It should be obvious by now that careers education and guidance is as complex and specialised an undertaking as any academic subject. There is no room for out–of–date, anecdotal, directive information and guidance, and senior staff are particularly prone to feeling that they have to express an opinion on almost everything, and to appear to have the answers to student and parental inquiries at their fingertips. Careers teaching requires continuity as much as any subject, and the frequent and sometimes unavoidable calls on senior staff are not conducive to a well organised teaching strategy.

If they are going to join your teaching group, heads and deputies ought to attend some form of basic in–service training and if it isn't available, you must set it up yourself. When it comes to third–year exams and options for the fourth–year courses, the importance of having a head-teacher, director of studies and timetabler who are aware of the current vocational implications of course choice will be self–evident, and any efforts on your part to develop awareness of these implications among the staff will be well rewarded.

If you are fortunate in having a head and deputies who really are more experienced in the use of careers education and guidance skills than you are, then count your blessings, learn from them and decide how best to involve them in your programme, but remember that no one is in danger of becoming out of date in terms of knowledge of opportunities, as fast as a 'careers specialist'.

Schools industry liaison officers

In some LEAs, staff have been appointed with the express responsibility for encouraging and developing links between schools and industry. This may include some or all of the following:

1 arranging work experience programmes
2 arranging industrial placements of anything from two weeks to a year, for teachers
3 co-ordinating schools and industry working parties
4 compiling lists of employers who are prepared to arrange visits for school parties, or to visit schools to talk to parents, staff and pupils, or to assist in other ways with careers or subject–based programmes
5 arranging placements in schools and colleges for industrialists
6 liaison with MSC and industry training boards.

In some authorities these functions are the responsibility of the careers service. If there is a SILO in your authority then the resource which he/she represents for your careers programme is self–evident. As a point of contact with local employers – large and small – SILOs are invaluable. Whilst industrialists are only too aware of the benefits which can accrue in the long run from dialogue with, and participation in, schools they would often prefer to work through a central agency rather than have frequent, random and often conflicting requests from individual schools.

Project Trident co-ordinators

Project Trident is a scheme designed to bring together the resources of LEAs, voluntary organisations and industry, in order to provide young people up to the age of 19 with the following three 'prongs' of the Trident programme:

1 work experience
2 community service
3 residential courses for challenging pursuits.

The Trident Trust – funded by donations from industry and charitable trusts, and subventions from the DES and the Department of Industry – arranges for seconded project co-ordinators from industry, and the LEA provides an office and a project assistant. The co-ordinator acts as a central organiser providing local schools with opportunities for their pupils to become involved in any or all of the three elements of the scheme. The project represents an ideal way of enabling schools to use community resources to achieve some of the objectives which we have already placed at the core of the educational process.

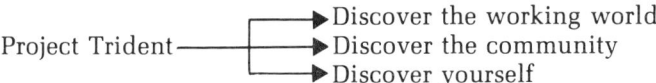

Project Trident ─────────→ Discover the working world
                       ├──→ Discover the community
                       └──→ Discover yourself

Educational welfare officers; educational psychologists; the schools medical service

All of these regular visitors to the school can be incorporated in the careers education programme to give information about their employment roles, the training they underwent, their job satisfactions and frustrations, and to provide a link with the designated careers adviser in their office. They also provide information – where it is possible for them to do so – about aspects of a student's home circumstances, medical history or personality and learning aptitudes, which may affect vocational choice. Hearing tests and tests of eyesight, colour vision and manual dexterity, may all be crucial in determining what is, or is not, open to a student. As we have already seen, up–to–date information about asthma, hay fever, arthritis or spinal curvature can prove equally important.

The integration of children with quite severe physical or educational disability into schools will mean that careers teachers and medical staff will have to work closely to determine what educational and vocational opportunities are, and should be, available to individual students. Educational psychologists may assist with the administration of aptitude and personality tests and can help you to consider the strengths and limitations of the tests which we will be looking at in a later section.

Voluntary agencies and the churches

Local community centres, youth clubs, community service volunteers, the churches and national charities like the NSPCC and the RSPCA represent major resources for teaching about the community and different roles within it. All of these organisations offer opportunities to give and to experience the satisfactions and frustrations of service. They are all prepared to give talks about their organisations and the work which they do, and many of them are trained in the techniques of group work and would be delighted to join or to lead a session with you and your students. To give just one example – your regional NSPCC inspector will almost certainly be prepared to:

– explain the work of the NSPCC and of individual inspectors
– outline the qualities needed for this work and the training given
– join classes discussing child care and parenthood
– organise a flag day using volunteers from your students
– provide opportunities for service experience in an NSPCC hostel for students living close to one.

Similar examples of education and involvement in the community could easily be given for any of the voluntary bodies. If your local authority doesn't do it, it would be a worthwhile experience to hold a convention of voluntary organisations in your school, or shared between local schools. If religious education, careers education and personal and social development are to mean anything more than an academic exercise then it is this kind of community involvement which schools should be developing – and many are.

Employers
Private industry and commerce

One of the catalysts of the Great Education Debate was the often–publicised complaint that employers were not reaping the benefits of the educational system in the form of appropriately educated, skilled and well–motivated school leavers. One of the fruitful outcomes of the debate has been the growth of school/industry liaison and a willingness on the part of both schools and employers to consider each other's aims, problems and needs, and to seek practical solutions wherever possible.

Even in this difficult economic climate there is ample evidence of the willingness of employers to contribute to *well–organised* school programmes.

Groups of employers and their representatives

Professional bodies   Many professional bodies maintain careers advisers, or panels of members throughout the country, who are prepared to visit schools for conventions, group talks, or to introduce films. All of the bodies produce careers literature and deal with specific enquiries. Many of them hold their own conventions for students and their careers staff.
Industrial training boards   There has been a reduction in the number of training boards representing individual industries, but those that remain are a useful source of information about levels of entry, abilities sought,

methods and duration of training, and the advantages of sandwich courses and sponsorship.

Local associations   Chambers of Commerce, Junior Chambers of Commerce, and local employers' associations have always been a useful source of information about local industry and commerce. Many of them are now managing agents for the MSC's Youth Training Scheme and could assist in explaining the scheme to your fifth year students, perhaps attending a broad careers convention of the type described in a later section.

Rotary Clubs, Round Tables and the Soroptimists – their female equivalent – in addition to their charitable work, often form panels of speakers covering their different occupations and are frequently prepared to provide 'mock interviews' for school leavers as part of the schools' careers programme. Because of their essentially local character they are an obvious source of work experience and can also help older students form a clearer conception of a career they might be seriously considering.

Schools and industry liaison groups   Many LEAs have regular meetings of representatives of education, industry and commerce, some of which are formally structured and highly organised. Co-ordination of the group is sometimes through an LEA adviser or education officer and occasionally through a SILO or careers officer. The work of various working parties may cover any of the following areas:

– discussion of existing curriculum, philosophy and practice, and proposed changes
– discussion of the structure, training and manpower needs of local firms, and significant national trends
– discussion of the acceptability of various examination grades for recruitment to training and employment
– exchange visits between teachers and employers
– work experience programmes, with specific reference to improving their effectiveness
– the provision of curricular material across the whole range of employment–related awareness and skills
– examination of methods of recruitment and moves towards common selection tests. Moves to improve transfer from school or college to employment, or youth training, and to improve induction procedures.
– the provision of information about local industry and commerce in lessons, at conventions and through local directories
– liaison with regional and national bodies and the involvement of projects like the 'Understanding British Industry' project, and the Industrial Society's 'Challenge of Industry' sixth–form conferences.
– liaison with university and polytechnic departments.

If your authority has a school and industry liaison group, find out what practical resources they have to offer and keep yourself up to date with their work.

Individual employers

The point has already been made about using established schemes within an authority to make contact with employers willing to help schools and colleges. The range of services which they can provide to enrich learning experiences has also been covered. The advantage of building a regular working relationship with certain employers is, of course, that you don't have to go repeatedly through the whole procedure of breaking the ice, explaining your aims and objectives, examining the possibilities, and agreeing a strategy and tactics. The advantages of continuity for a busy careers teacher can't be overstressed. It also means that your energies can be put into improving on the work you do together.

The disadvantages are that you might come to rely on too few contacts, and become too narrow in your involvement of adults other than teachers. It might also be that they will find the arrangement becoming an increasing burden on their time as one – or both of you – begins to get carried away with understandable enthusiasm.

A more serious problem to be aware of is the building up – consciously or otherwise – of favoured recruitment. Strong links with a particular school, an appreciation of what it is trying to achieve, and an opportunity to work with and observe students in their final year at school or college can tempt an employer to make a direct approach to a school or individual careers teacher rather than notifying the careers office or advertising in the local press. The advantages for the employer are that he is able to vet potential applicants in advance and is assured of a steady flow of suitable talent. The school will have a 'better' record of school–leaver employment, and in theory everybody gains.

In practice, however, the method is both unfair and unwise. One school in England, until quite recently, provided the bulk of the craft apprentices for a major employer in its locality, year after year, because of close links between the training officer and the careers teacher. Not only was this unfair to equally–able and possibly better–suited students in other schools, but it was also doing a disservice to many of the selected students who had the potential to pursue their studies to A–level and honours degree level. Nor is the 'I'll find you a good lad' syndrome confined to boys alone. Requests to send a selection of girls along for clerical and secretarial interviews are occasionally made direct to schools. Students sent along for interview under these circumstances find themselves under great pressure not to refuse offers of employment even when they feel that it would be in their best interest to refuse.

No careers teacher should ever agree to support this practice. All offers should be politely received as flattering to the school and its students and then redirected to the careers office with friendly and firm explanation. Most employers are aware of the code of practice which is agreed by LEAs and employers' associations, and the work of schools/industry liaison should include the publicising of these codes.

These dangers apart, the involvement of employers can only enhance your work, provided that you follow the guidelines suggested and take up the examples of good practice exemplified in the School's Council Industry Project.

Public services

The Civil Service, Social Services and local government departments may be prepared to help with units of work which deal with the role of these services in the economy, and some of the responsibilities of citizenship. In a more direct way, the Inland Revenue and Department of Health and Social Security issue to schools pamphlets which explain the intricacies of paying tax for the first time and of applying for social security allowances. As employers, they are prepared to discuss vocational prospects and work roles, and some work experience may be provided. The highly confidential nature of some of the work will tend to restrict the number of placements offered.

The police force, fire and ambulance services, probationary service and local health visitors are all excellent resources for careers education. They are all concerned to develop the preventative aspect of their work – as far as time and personnel will allow – and in doing so they will also be broadening the students' concepts of this job family, developing a sense of personal and communal responsibility, and an understanding of service in a vocational context.

They are also a source of work and community experience through voluntary cadet schemes, play groups, and community self–help projects.

Trade unions

No examination of British industry could possibly be complete without the inclusion of trade unions. Fear of appearing to reflect political bias has prevented too many schools from making use of trade union officials in careers education. There is no reason for supposing that a trade union official should be more capable of showing political bias than an employer. By bringing both together, in order to set up simulations of good and bad industrial relations in the classroom, we stand a better chance of enabling this generation to understand and begin to solve some of the related problems, than by leaving our students to make sense of the edited highlights on the news.

The CRAC *Business Experience Case Studies* use this technique, but how much more effective if you had an employer and a shop steward playing the game with your students – reversing their roles perhaps – or acting as observers and joining in the de–briefing sessions.

Safety at work is one area in which the trade union movement has become an expert, and serious and professional examination of the future of work and of leisure – which has already been alluded to in this book – shows the breadth of concern of union leaders like Clive Jenkins and full–time research officials like Barrie Sherman.

Utilise the resources of the trade unions but, as with any other resource, think carefully about how you would like to involve them.

Universities, polytechnics, colleges and institutes of further and higher education

During the 1960s and early 1970s there was a rapid expansion of the number of places available in further and higher education, in response to post–war birth rates and rising educational aspirations. Rationalisation of teacher-training and other courses with falling secondary rolls in mind, and a desire to encourage technological and 'vocational' courses at the expense of arts and humanities by selective cuts in funding, has left some courses and institutions over–subscribed, and others vying for the most able students or fighting to keep their courses viable.

Apart from the effects outlined in Part 1 (see pages 16/7), this means that would–be applicants have to be even better informed than ever before about the nature of courses, standards of entry, vocational and other implications of courses, and even the viability of certain institutions and courses. Fortunately, the institutions themselves are equally mindful both of their responsibilities and their need to attract able students, and the following resources are commonly available:

– prospectuses and course details
– visits and lectures from admissions tutors
– visits and lectures from subject tutors
– visits from members of the students' union
– individual and group visits to institutions
– attendance at careers conventions and higher education forums
– alternative prospectuses issued by the students' union
– film and video prospectuses
– day and residential courses for sixth–formers
– conferences for subject and careers teachers/careers officers
– willingness to become involved with school–based projects
– *Schools liaison officers* to co-ordinate most of the above.

This is one area where the sheer volume of information and assistance is such that I would urge you to:

1 Set up systems which enable your students to find out as much of what they need to discover, for themselves. (See the section on the careers library.)
2 Encourage your academic subject colleagues to make use of the visits and lectures available, and keep them up to date on the most significant changes in their field.

While it is generally accepted that the universities, polytechnics and colleges and institutes of higher education offer these services in a spirit of altruism – calculating that they will get their fair share of applicants and that they will tend to be better informed and more highly motivated as a result – colleges of further education and sixth form and tertiary colleges are too often viewed with suspicion. They are totally dependent upon local students and they may well be in a competitive position vis à vis each other, or local sixth forms, but this is no justification for failing to take advantage of all of the opportunities for co-operation, liaison and dissemination of information. You will have the responsibility, however, for insisting upon an honest and unbiased presentation at all times – apart from being essential for your students, in the long run it's in the interest of the FE institution as well.

Science And Technology Regional Organisations (SATROs)

There are 25 or so SATROs throughout the country. To quote their own literature, they exist to:

> '. . . encourage a modern approach to science and technology in schools, to improve understanding amongst schools, industry, commerce and government agencies, and to provide practical help in developing co-operative activities between the world of education and the world of work.'

Operated as charitable trusts and funded by industry, commerce and government agencies, the management committees of SATROs usually consist of equal numbers of representatives of industry and commerce on the one hand, and education on the other. The methods by which they seek to meet their objectives include:
– compilation of information directories
– programmed visits
– development of curriculum materials
– meetings
– conferences
– submissions to royal commissions and government inquiries
– liaison with other bodies – Equal Opportunities Commission, Women in Engineering, Engineering Careers Information Office

Some of the areas of the curriculum with which the author's local SATRO – the Centre for Industry, Science, Technology, Education Liaison based at Manchester Polytechnic – is concerned are the implication of the applications of microelectronics for society, the response of the primary school curriculum to the above, using microcomputers to help the physically handicapped pupil, and opportunities for girls to enjoy, develop and see the relevance of scientific and technological skills to future opportunities in engineering and other technologies.

There is a lot of scope here for involving your colleagues in the sciences, maths and design departments, in addition to the obvious applications in a careers programme.

i(c) **Other resources**
The students themselves
It's easy to forget, but important not to, that the students are a fund of information about themselves, and the people and world around them. Self–awareness, problem–solving, decision–making and all of the skills-related work, would be impossible without the students' input. Role–play, simulations and case studies, work experience feedback, interview techniques: so much of the work requires their interaction and experience. In this subject they have to become their own major resource by the time they leave you. Active rather than passive, self–directing rather than directed. This ought to be reflected in the extent to which your lessons depend upon their participation.

Ancillary staff
All of the non–teaching staff in a school could contribute to your pro-gramme. The students see them about their work without ever reflecting upon what it is really like, what training was required, what other activities or occupations these people engage in for money, relaxation, pleasure or out of a sense of responsibility.

If you begin to involve caretakers, office staff, cleaners, welfare assis-tants and laboratory technicians in your programme, by using question-naires, taped or videotaped interviews, you'll find there are a number of pleasing side effects:
– students gain a better understanding of the nature of work which they see going on around them
– they take the support services in the school much less for granted
– they begin to relate to ancillary staff as people rather than just as workers, and greater courtesy and co-operation become evident
– the attitude of ancillary staff towards the students mellows, and there is a greater sense of community and common purpose.

In small schools and in primary schools ancillary staff are often able to feel part of the community, and students unconsciously learn from their contact with, and observation of, these adults other than teachers. In a larger school it can be facilitated by involving them in the careers or personal and social education programmes.

Past pupils
Whenever past pupils are encouraged to share their experiences since leaving school with those still at school, there is a noticeable rise in the interest and concentration shown by students. This is hardly surprising because they know that these ex–pupils – the brothers and sisters of many of their peers – have only recently gone through the transition which they are about to make.

Although it is not uncommon for students in higher education to be asked back to school to talk about life at university, polytechnic and college, it is rare for ex–pupils to be asked to discuss further education, employment, YTS and unemployment in the same way. Fear of bias, exaggeration, and misrepresentation tend to be used to discourage the use of ex–pupils in this way, but such claims fail to credit our ex–students and existing students with the ability to discriminate and to be honest.

Providing that they are well briefed, and that you monitor and follow up these sessions, they can be among the most rewarding of all external resources. Since older brothers and sisters, and friends, are already a powerful influence on the decisions made by your students, why not show that you recognise the fact, and use them to enrich and reinforce your programme? One of the hidden benefits is that students see that they continue to be valued by the school after they have left, and the personal, social and community aspects of that realisation are invaluable.

Parents

The wealth of evidence that parents often play the most significant part in option choices at 14 +, and especially in the decision to seek employment or to enter further education at 16, means that it is essential that they are aware of what the school is trying to achieve and have the opportunity to assist in the process wherever they can. They have a right to be so involved.

Our responsibility is to see that parents understand the implications of course choices; are aware of the range of opportunities open to their children appropriate to their ability and aspirations; have the opportunity to attend parents' evenings, careers interviews and careers conventions, well briefed and conspicuously welcome; know what the careers programme is aiming to achieve and how and when they can help.

In return, parents can help in a number of ways. One of the nagging pressures on fourth–, fifth– and even sixth–form students is the frequent question posed by parents, relatives and friends: 'What are you going to do when you leave school?' Evasive and uncertain answers inevitably bring the retort, 'You'd better go and see the careers teacher, hadn't you?' The fact that regular careers lessons and a pattern of interviews have already helped to narrow the options to as fine a degree as would be appropriate for this student at this time, is unlikely to emerge. Apart from being reluctant to reveal their tentative plans in case the parental approval which they often desperately want is not forthcoming, there is often a feeling – which schools may unconsciously foster – that they wouldn't understand anyway. If parents were actively involved they would stand a better chance of understanding – and they might be able to help, where before they simply appeared to nag.

- Encourage your students to show and discuss their career file with their parents.
- Use questionnaires on areas like work and non-work roles, job satisfaction, leisure pursuits, attitudes to retirement and equal opportunities to involve parents in the careers education programme.
- Ask students to check their own self–assessments with their parents as

well as their friends. Students are usually very honest and often over-critical when assessing themselves, and it is nice to give parents the chance to bolster their confidence, and to encourage them to consider skills which they have, but do not recognise.

– Parents can help with rough drafts of application forms and often encourage students to mention interests or activities which adolescent modesty would otherwise discount.

These are relatively simple but very effective ways of developing a sense of partnership between school, parent and child in a very difficult process. Involving parents in group work or talks during lesson time to make use of their particular experiences as employers, employees, voluntary workers, housewives and so on is perfectly feasible provided that the checklist for all visiting speakers is followed and that their children are comfortable with the idea of having their mother or father involved in this way. There are enough examples of schools and colleges where parents take O–levels and A–levels and other courses alongside their children, to set a precedent for 'all age' careers lessons – and where better to use their experience?

Conclusion

People are a rich and underused resource in education. Try to move away from the static and didactic approach of lectures and isolated visits. Look at how you can develop case studies, simulations, role plays and problem–solving exercises. Wherever possible, get adults other than teachers involved in the lessons as equals with the students. Both will learn faster and far more effectively from this kind of interaction. One of the secrets behind the dramatic release of enthusiasm, creativity and accelerated learning which personal computers bring to young people – and to disabled children in particular – is the fact that the chidren have equality, or rather superiority, of status with the machine. They can go as far and as fast as they are able to, setting their own limits and following their own interests.

The traditional didactic method of education has certainly acted as a brake on intellectual and social development through its pattern of hierarchies, its emphasis on teacher and pupil, and the need to proceed broadly in line with the rest of the class. We tend to keep our children young, and the longer the period is before they are likely to enter regular employment the greater is the temptation to do so.

If sophisticated machine–based learning offers some liberation in intellectual development, it doesn't in the field of social development – at least not to the same degree. Try to use your adults to provide opportunities for students to explore for themselves, to be creative, to examine day–to–day problems at work, in the home, in the community, and to suggest solutions which may be implemented. A careers lesson on the role of a health visitor can result in the identification of special needs for the elderly, the involvement of the science department and school science club, and the development of a practical solution. In a Salford school just this kind of interaction has resulted in regular projects funded by the local authority.

The more adults other than teachers you use in a discriminating way, the more often will 'head' learning become 'heart' learning as well.

ii Places

ii(a) Careers specialist
Internal
The careers room
The careers library
Interview rooms
External
The careers office
Careers conventions

ii(b) Other resources
The lecture room
The drama theatre
The computer room
Specialist rooms
The teachers' centre
Places of further/higher education
Places of employment
Places of recreation
Places of voluntary work

Any place is a potential resource for careers education. Those listed above have the merit of being particularly useful, and their potential will depend on the people who control them, and with whom you liaise. As the previous section dealt at length with the use of people as a resource this section is concerned with the possibilities presented by the physical characteristics and organisations of these places. NB It is rare for a school to be blessed with *all* of the physical resources examined here, but since they are as important to you as science labs are to the physics department you should be aware of what is possible and worth bidding for.

ii(a) Careers specialist
The careers room   If you are fortunate enough to have a regular base, this is where the bulk of your lessons will be taught. The layout of the room in terms of flexibility of seating, storage space, displays, access or proximity to your office or an interview area, or the careers library, will all dictate the potential of the area as a learning resource. Serried rows, limited display and storage space will hardly set the scene for group work, role play, information–finding, and learning through participation. Decide how you intend to work and then design or rearrange the room accordingly. If

careers is infused throughout the curriculum then show colleagues how their rooms can be quickly rearranged to provide the appropriate setting for mock interviews, role plays or discussion groups. If the room provided is small, make out a case for the largest available classroom on the basis of the range of activities which you intend to use. Many careers teachers have a room which doubles up as the careers library and classroom, and in one case a head of careers who had waited in vain for years for a careers library and an interview area, removed the door from his stock room and transformed it into an office, storage area and information room, as an extension to his careers room.

Careers infusion can be used as an excuse for not having a careers teaching room or suite, but there is no excuse for not having a careers library.

The careers library

A vast amount of careers information arrives at schools throughout the year. Some of the information is repetitive but much of it is providing details of new courses, training opportunities, entry requirements, application procedures, and trends in employment. Sadly, the evidence from many careers teachers is that too much of this information does not reach them, arrives too late, or is misdirected. The absence of an organised careers library is the primary reason for this neglect.

If we intend to see that our students are well informed, become self–directive and have access to up–to–date information about their vocational choices, then we have to provide a suitable area for the storage and display of relevant information. It seems unsupportable that the provision of information about life choices should receive less priority than the building up of an existing stock of popular novels, but it frequently does. The irony is that the bulk of the careers information is free.

The major users of your careers library are going to be your students, yourself and members of staff. The priorities are that it should have an efficient system of classification, storage and retrieval, and that there should be adequate provision for display of material, and opportunities for browsing and detailed study of the information available.

Although it may seem a daunting prospect at first, there is no shortage of advice on how to proceed. COIC – Careers and Occupational Information Centre – have produced a slide and tape presentation entitled 'How to set up a careers library', which is certain to be available through your local careers service. In addition to providing hints on the use of space and methods of storage and display, it also suggests a method of organisation and explains careers library classification systems such as its own CLCI.

The CLCI – 'Careers Library Classification Index' – is the most widely–used system in larger libraries because this COIC/CRAC index system is increasingly being adopted by other bodies. Basically, the CLCI system groups the major fields of employment into 26 job families, each of which corresponds to a letter of the alphabet. Subdivisions within a job family are given an expanded code thus:

Finance and related work	
General information	N
Accountancy	NAB
Banking	NAD
Building societies	NAF

The advantage of this system is that it is possible to group job families, and thereby widen students' vocational horizons. Under this system, all of the paramedical careers will appear in close proximity to one another – often in the same box file – whilst under an alphabetical system they may be yards apart. It also means that literature which applies to the whole job family is easier to place. The concept of job families is also used by the MSC, although they use a different classification, and within the TVEI. There is no reason why your students shouldn't be able to master the CLCI system, provided that you give them practice through group and individual information finding projects.

A brief tour of the careers library which is presented in diagram 11 may help to indicate what to include, how to organise it, and how to use it. Although this is a model rather than an actual plan, it does represent an amalgam of three existing careers libraries – one of which has three interview rooms and offices leading off it. Nothing is impossible!

Diagram 11 The careers library

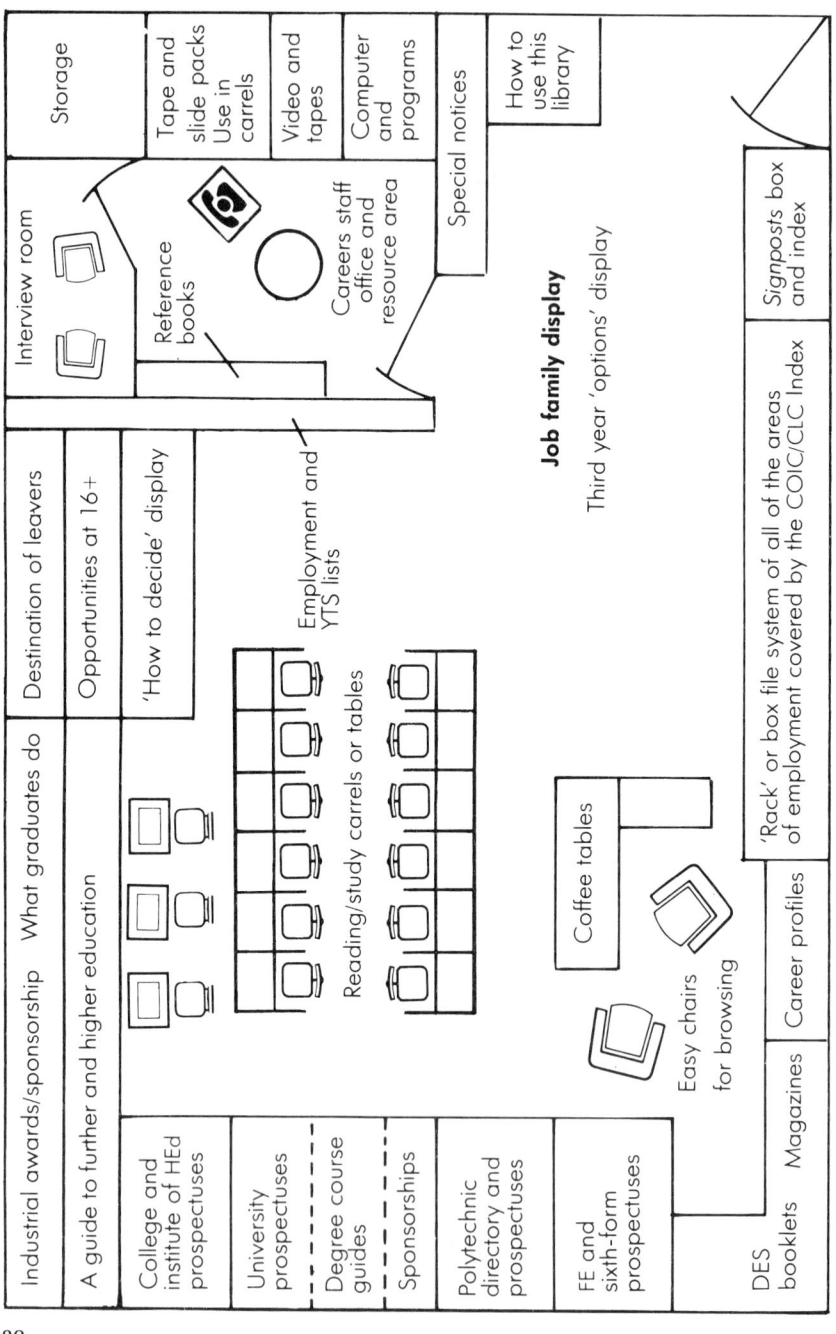

On entry, a wall display on the right explains the layout of the library and suggests how it may be used. Specific examples of a 'job search' and a 'course search' lead students through the questions they should put to themselves, and the places in the library where they can find the answers, in a sequenced flow diagram. A cassette version of these searches can be found among the computer programs in the resource area.

On the left of the door the *Signposts* box or card file index for the careers library classification can be found with an explanation of how to use the system, and a poster showing the 26 CLCI job families, and their subdivisions.

Along the same wall, a series of shelves support plastic or cardboard box files containing careers information – usually in leaflet or pamphlet form – about the various fields of employment, training or voluntary work. You can devise your own additions to cover other life choices or occupational information. All of this information follows the CLCI classification system – or your own alphabetical one.

Along the same wall, several shelves carry copies of individual career profiles in book or booklet form. Next to them a rack holds a range of magazines subscribed to by the school or careers department, or brought in by staff and students. Through links with local hospitals or the school nurse you might be able to scrounge copies of nursing magazines, and there is an abundance of reasonably–priced careers magazines ideal for sparking off interest in browsing sessions.

In this corner of the library, easy chairs and coffee tables are provided for browsing and relaxed reading and there are more beyond the study carrels.

Several tables or wall racks are used to display booklets distributed free by the Department of Education and Science, the Department of Health and Social Security, the Department of Employment and the Inland Revenue, covering the various decision points, grants and subsidies, courses, paying tax for the first time, and so on.

Four sets of filing cabinets – side by side – contain the prospectuses of all the local institutions offering 16–19 education, and the national universities, polytechnics, colleges and institutes of further and higher education. Sections of the cabinets are reserved for further information about higher education, including degree course guides, sponsorships, a year off, alternative prospectuses and so on.

Along the adjoining wall, sections are reserved for displays of posters and diagrams highlighting areas of particular interest in higher education, further education and training, and graduate and post–training opportunities.

One section is taken up by a permanent display of opportunities at 16+, destination of past leavers, and decision–making strategies.

The whole of the chipboard wall, used to create the careers office, is given over to a display of current employment, training, and YTS lists issued by local employers, the MSC managing agents, and the careers service.

In the centre of the room, reading and study carrels – or tables – provide for quiet reading and study of the information available in the library, or for fifth form/sixth form private study. This has the advantage of enabling careful scrutiny of information without having to remove it from the library, helps to create a purposive atmosphere conducive to serious consideration of the material, and helps you to justify the use of a comparatively large area for these purposes. There will be times of the day – perhaps at lunchtimes or in the mornings before registration – when you want to encourage browsing and relaxed use of the library, but this is quite different from allowing it to be used like a common room or shelter from wet breaks.

Near the door is a standing display board which can be used for weekly or fortnightly displays – perhaps to complement or reinforce a topic in the careers education or guidance programme – a job family, third year option, or guide to the careers convention display would come under this heading. It is important with these displays that they should be brought to the attention of relevant students in a positive way – at assemblies or in careers lessons – and changed regularly as appropriate.

Opposite the door, a noticeboard containing special notices, careers interview lists or careers bulletins stands outside the careers office and resource area.

The careers office and resource area is where the careers staff do their administrative work, keep their teaching and learning resources, and give guidance to individual students or parents. One desk at least – with trays for correspondence, references, incoming material – is essential. The telephone is also a vital piece of equipment. If the education and guidance systems outlined in this book are implemented, it is likely that the careers co-ordinator will make and receive more calls than any other member of the staff, with the possible exception of the head.

Copies of all of the major compendiums and handbooks will be available for students in the library area but careers advisers' reference texts will be stored in the shelves in the office.

Ideally, there should be a separate interview room where careers interviews and guidance interviews can be carried out without the inevitable interruptions of ringing phones and knocks on the door. Nothing is calculated to undermine a sensitive interview more than heads popping round the door at frequent intervals. It also means that the careers officer has a regular and appropriate place for interviews in close proximity to the careers staff, and this facilitates briefing and debriefing.

Storage for audio/visual material used in the careers programme could be in a freestanding cupboard or filing cabinet; the students should have access to tape and slide packs for individual use with headphones in the study carrels. Providing that the room is secure, a videorecorder and television monitor – used jointly with the careers computer – will be in the office with all of the careers tapes, home–made as well as purchased.

Finally, a microcomputer in the APPLE, BBC, Commodore PET or 380Z range, complete with tapes, is available for use with the *Careers on Computer* series, for access to databases like the Prestel careers data, or for storing and accessing careers records and data.

If all of this seems fanciful, then it is unlikely that you will ever achieve it. If you accept it as an attainable ideal worth fighting for, then you have every chance of succeeding. The capital expense is going to be one five-hundredth of the cost of a sports hall; every student will benefit from it as an information and learning resource, and the skills acquired in using it will last a lifetime.

One thing that falling rolls are bringing is space. Fight for your share! If the Parent Teachers' Association are prepared to work to provide a swimming pool or a set of tennis courts, how much more willing will they be to subsidise a careers library?

A careers library deserves ancillary support in the form of a librarian, but many school systems depend upon trained library monitors or prefects from among the students, which turned out to be initial training for one of our careers officers!

Once your library is organised you can *use it in the following ways* :
– introductory tours of the library for class groups
– quizzes, questionnaires and competitions to test and reinforce knowledge of how to use the library
– programmed searches based on *SPEEDCOP*, job family, job and higher education searches
– individual research for personal vocational develoment
– browsing general interest sessions, to broaden horizons and stimulate.

In addition to gaining the information they need to make decisions while they are at school, your students should also have learned how to use a library and the resources associated with it – including up–to–date information technology – to help them to make decisions after they have made the transition from school.

The careers office

Ideally, all of your students should receive an introduction to the careers office – as well as the school's careers officer – before they leave school. The full range of services, the systems which operate there, the need for regular contact, the limitations of the service, the information displayed in the office – all of these can best be explained by a visit or a video, through programmes filmed by a team of careers teachers and officers, possibly with the assistance of students. There are a number of careers offices which have produced their own guides on video tape, and the author's local careers workshop – consisting of careers teachers and officers – is engaged on its own video film at present. When it is completed it should make it easier for the students to use the careers office efficiently, without too many qualms, and serve the subsidiary function of showing an office–based service at work.

Careers conventions

In *Practical Approaches to Careers Education* (CRAC/Hobsons, 1978) Catherine Avent provided a most searching analysis of careers conventions. If you intend to hold one then it is recommended that you read Chapter 11 of that book.

Whilst Miss Avent deals with all of the principles and practicalities involved, it is noticeable that the limitations are given detailed coverage, and the advantages are difficult to find. This is because the useful role of a careers convention can be summed up as:

– An opportunity for students and their parents to meet the representatives of employers, occupations, and institutions of further and higher education, in order to gain and clarify information about future opportunities.

This can only be achieved against a background of a thorough and continuing programme of careers education in a school. Too often they are organised against a background of limited careers education, treated as a public relations exercise on behalf of the school, and looked upon as the primary means of providing vocational information. Parents frequently come with the expectation that they will be able to seek and receive guidance on an individual basis – something which is impossible and unwise given the numbers attending, and the limited knowledge of the students on the part of the visitors.

The objectives of a careers convention can best be achieved – and far more economically for careers staff and visitors alike – by involving the same visitors in a careers programme in the ways suggested in the previous section. If you have been covering one of the job families in the careers programme, invite the visitors, students and parents to an evening meeting to follow up the school–based sessions. This is more valuable, more controllable and more meaningful an exercise than a full scale jamboree run by a school which has a minimal careers programme and no careers library.

If there is a place for large–scale conventions at present then it might be along the lines of those provided at some local centre like the technical or tertiary college, or the town hall, covering sources of local employment and training, leisure and voluntary organisations. These are available to the whole community – not just schoolchildren or the few schools which have the resources to run a convention – and they fulfil the function of bringing a wide sweep of opportunities to the attention of those who attend.

One of the disadvantages which has not existed before is that you will have to include Youth Training Schemes in an employer–based convention, and there is greater temptation for using the convention as a recruitment exercise on the part of a training organisation which stands to lose financially for each place unfilled on the scheme. It is even more essential that information about these schemes is given in a controlled and impartial setting. I believe that all of the options at 16+ have to be presented positively, and that any course of training or further education is likely to be of greater benefit to a school–leaver than the prospect of a lengthy period without it, but misrepresentation or ill–conceived guidance is a real danger.

Bring potential trainers into the careers programme in the same way that employers are involved, and follow the same procedure of establishing the ground rules and principles first. An honest examination of what is offered can only be helpful to all involved.

If you already have a well organised careers structure in the school, then you may wish to complement it with a convention, but if you haven't, you may prefer to put your valuable time and energy into building up a programme which involves these resources in a more productive way.

ii(b) Other resources

The lecture room may prove ideal for large scale lectures, film and video screenings when time is limited, and illustrated talks.

The drama theatre is an ideal setting for some simulations and games, and may have a studio attached for making/editing video and tape recordings.

The computer room may be where your computerised careers programs will have to be used at first, and is also a source of initial introduction to keyboard skills and computer literacy.

Specialist rooms ought to have their own displays of careers–related information, visiting speakers/demonstrators/'joining the class' visitors, and may be used for 'careers' work in a programme of 'infusion'.

External resources: places of employment, training, and education, leisure and voluntary work, in addition to offering the resources already dealt with under 'people', and to be dealt with under 'things', are unique in being able to provide visits and work experience.

Work visits

There are a number of different motives for arranging visits to places of employment, and these include:

- reinforcement of a topic studied in a specialist lesson, eg visit to a weaving or spinning mill in a history lesson; to a nuclear power station in a physics lesson; to a sewage processing works in an environmental science lesson; to a bank in an economics lesson
- to undertake a detailed study of one organisation to discover how it functions
- to enable a student intending to embark on a particular 'career' to sample the work which would be involved initially, and to observe how it might develop
- to enable a group of students to gain some insight into the nature of one particular job family through a number of separate visits to different institutions.

Each of these reasons for arranging a visit will have its own specific objectives and it is a mistake to try to achieve too many different aims in one visit. Topic reinforcement by subject staff will have some impact on the students' occupational awareness. It is useful for the careers staff to be aware of the visits made by different subject staff and to help in finding appropriate places of employment for other departments to visit.

Detailed study of one institution is not really feasible with a large group of students, but a small team, well briefed and hopefully armed with a video camera, could produce an excellent project which would form the basis of discussion and examination for all of the other students. This would be a useful resource for a number of years, as well as a learning experience for the students involved. You do need impeccable relations with the employer, probably built up through a successful partnership in the provision of work experience.

Job sampling is always a risk in the sense that no student visiting a firm for a short period of time, or even working for a long summer holiday, can really experience a job in the sense that one would as a permanent, trained, adult employee. Nevertheless, there is a place for occasional individual placements during weekends or holiday periods for younger students, and during private study or extension study time for sixth formers, *provided that careful preparation and de-briefing takes place*. These placements can become positive motivators, and can be helpful in deciding a student against a course of action which was based on romantic notions of, for example, 'nursing' or 'architecture'. They should be under no misconceptions that the life of a Nurse Class 2 (formerly an SRN) is like that of a voluntary helper, which is what they will have experienced, or that life in a small architects' office is typical of the profession as a whole and useful preparation for a degree course at university.

Visits to a range of institutions can be very helpful in making comparisons and filling out occupational impressions, but are also costly in terms of time, effort, and absence from the lessons of colleagues whose courses will have been as carefully and tightly structured as your own. One way around this is to organise different visits for different groups of students in the same term and then let each team describe and comment on their impressions of their own visit for the benefit of the other groups. This has the added advantage of giving a focus to careful observation and recording of information during the visits, and reinforcing communication skills afterwards. Judicious use of video cameras – again with permission agreed in advance – can help make up for the limit on the number of visits.

Work experience

Work experience is an opportunity for students to find out what it is like to have a job to do in a place of adult employment. As far as possible – allowing for their lack of training, and taking their safety and that of their workmates into account – they will follow a normal work pattern, but without being paid. Where this is not possible they are likely to spend a certain amount of time in each of the departments, performing simple tasks, and observing the regular employees.

Purpose

1 It may be considered as a vehicle for preparing young people for the transition from full–time education to employment, or to employment–related training. Considering that education is a preparation for adult life, and that employment is going to continue to play a major role in adult life well into the foreseeable future, it seems only right that education should work with employment to provide some direct experience to ease the transition from one to the other – however long the gap might be, for some students, between the unpaid and the paid experience.

2 Work experience is a learning situation in which students can use and develop the whole range of skills and awareness defined in the objectives of careers education. Coping, information, communication, decision–making and problem–solving skills will all be brought into play during a short spell in a new and challenging environment. This is also an ideal situation in which to examine their own self–concept, to observe at first hand other people's vocational identities, and to consider their own developing occupational concept. If this seems to be a rather extravagant claim, consider this example:

Jane Doe   Age: 15 years 3 months
Work experience placement: Town hall reception

Jane has one younger sister, has babysat a few times, but has never had a part–time or holiday job. She is quiet, hardworking and has a few firm friends. She is expected to achieve five moderate CSE grades next summer and is unlikely to stay on at school although she may apply for a secretarial course in the sixth form, or at the local tertiary college.

For the next three weeks Jane has to make her own way to the town hall. She has to cope with meeting a large number of new people – all of them older than her – some of whom she will be working closely with. She is responsible for her own transport arrangements, snacks and lunch arrangements, and has to decide whether or not to join the section tea and coffee fund. There is a lot to remember at first about clocking in and out, cloakrooms and toilets, where the different offices are, fire regulations, use of the telephone for private calls, who to contact in case of illness or emergency, and lots and lots of names.

The first task she is given is fairly straightforward – sorting the mail. The mail trays are organised on a departmental basis. The trouble is that many of the letters are addressed to individuals rather than departments, and some simply say 'The Town Hall'. The other clerical staff are used to the system and chat as they work; Jane has to interrupt them frequently at first but begins to get the hang of it by the second day.

As a means of helping her to familiarise herself with the different offices she is asked to help take the coffee and biscuits round for the mid–morning break. She is a little worried about interrupting important meetings but she needn't have worried; the only disaster is when she spills a cup of tea on the carpet in the council chamber. Fortunately, there is a cleaner in the corridor and she shows Jane where the mops are kept. Everyone is very nice about it, but Jane can't help wondering what it would have been like if this had been her first day in a 'real' job.

The other tasks she is introduced to during that first week include sorting out alphabetical files, weeding out old ones and running errands between departments. She discovers that she has quite a talent for spotting the right name from among a long list of names, and quickly picks up the filing systems as well. She also finds out that carrying verbal messages is a lot harder than carrying written ones.

Now that she knows her way around the Town Hall she is put on reception for the whole of the second week. Most of the time there is a regular receptionist there to help her, but as she becomes more confident she finds that she is left increasingly on her own. This means handling difficult – sometimes irate – members of the public as well as pleasant ones, directing them to the right departments, taking messages and checking whether people are available by using the internal phone. There are times when she is confused, flustered, embarrassed; other times when she is amused and even flattered. Some of the time she finds that she has very little to do and is bored. By the end of the third week she is surprised at how confidently she has managed to cope with all of the tasks she has been given, but is glad to be going back to school.

Apart from the tasks described above, Jane has also been required by her careers teacher to keep a daily log of her activities, her feelings, and anything which she feels she has learnt during the course of the day. She also has specific questions to ask of her workmates, and of the personnel manager responsible for her during her placement. She shows her file to the personnel manager and writes a letter of thanks for the help she has been given.

Back at school she discusses her file with the careers teacher, and is asked to share her experiences with the rest of the class, as they will with her, in a controlled discussion and de–briefing.

It doesn't take a lot of imagination to see how this experience can prove to be a useful learning experience for Jane. The benefits normally ascribed to work experience *conducted in this way* are that it has the effect of:
– *Deepening understanding of the world of work* in many ways, but especially in terms of the nature of tasks; methods of organisation; roles and status; social interaction; methods of selection, training, and opportunities for professional advancement; the different forms of stress attached to certain tasks, discipline and self-discipline, different forms of job satisfaction or methods of coping with monotony or boredom. Just how many of these aspects of work are understood, or how well assimilated, depends on the nature of the placement, the quality of preparation and follow–up provided by the careers teacher, and the learning capacity of the student. The same is true of all of the other possible benefits.

- *Stimulating greater interest in personal vocational planning.*
- *Encouraging better motivation towards school work and willingness to consider further study beyond 16.*
- *Developing greater self-confidence and maturity* as a result of acceptance by adults in an adult situation; the ability to cope with the tasks set, and to succeed in a non–school situation.

All of these benefits are recognised by careers staff in schools with a systematic approach to work experience, and in countries where it is an integral part of the high school curriculum it has been claimed that even more substantial periods of work experience have no detrimental effect on school work, and frequently improve attitudes towards school–based learning among less academically able students.

Organisation

Most local education authorities now have a policy regarding the provision of work experience. As stated earlier, co-ordination of local schemes is likely to be through one of the following: the careers office, Project Trident co-ordinators, an education department co-ordinator, a schools and industry liaison working party.

Whichever system is used, it takes a tremendous burden away from individual careers teachers who have enough to do making the internal arrangements and preparing and de-briefing students, without having to worry about finding sympathetic and co-operative employers every year. The task of finding placements is hard enough for the full time co-ordinators, especially now that YTS and TVEI make their own considerable claims on employer co-operation.

It is worth mentioning at this point that the introduction of the Youth Training Scheme has not yet offered an alternative to school–based work experience. YTS experience will vary according to the nature of the particular scheme, but will often tend to be job specific – even though transferable skills are required – particularly where it replaces an apprenticeship scheme. Furthermore, since YTS is not available to those students who decide to continue in full–time education beyond the eligible age for acceptance on a scheme, there are 30% of each year group who would miss out on the opportunity to gain some work experience.

Given that external organisation is almost exclusively centralised, what follows concentrates on what you as a careers teacher will have to do inside the school. If you happen to be in an authority which has no central scheme, it is suggested that you refer to the checklist on the section dealing with 'People' as a resource, and use this in your approach to employers, together with the advice offered in for example the CRAC teachers' *Handbook on Work Experience*, and the SCIP booklet, *Work Experience in the School Curriculum*.

Preparation

1 Determine school policy with the headmaster. Agree the number and range of students, and the timing and duration of placements within the limits set by the LEA. (Some authorities encourage all fourth or fifth year students to participate – even to the extent of setting up or buying factories for the sole purpose – others may limit the numbers per school, or have to limit them according to the number of employers participating.)

2 Ensure that heads of department are aware of the agreed policy, and the purpose and benefits of the scheme.

3 Canvass those students who are eligible for the scheme, and ensure that they and their parents are aware of the nature and purpose of the scheme. Stress that it is not job tasting, training or the first stage in placement.

4 Place those students who have applied, giving them as much choice as possible, but stressing that any placement will meet the aims of the scheme.

5 Complete the forms which provide details of the placement for the pupil and those which provide details of the pupil and give parental consent, for the employer.

6 Inform all staff of the students and dates involved well in advance.

7 Throughout this period you should have been preparing the students for their work experience, and familiarising them with the work booklets or files which they will be required to keep during the placement.

8 Immediately before they begin their placement the students should be briefed, and a check made that they know how and when to arrive, the arrangements made for lunches, breaks and expenses, and who to contact at work and at school in case of an emergency or illness.

9 During the placements it is ideal, but often impossible, for you or your colleagues to visit the students. In many schools, more than 100 students may be on work experience in a short space of time. In this case it would be an idea to visit selectively those employers with whom you have never made contact, and those students who may need some support or monitoring.

10 At the end of the period, students will show their work books to the employer, thank them for their time and help orally and then by letter, and discuss their work books and experiences in careers lessons. Discussing them with their subject teachers might also improve the understanding of work experience and its value among your fellow staff.

Models

There are many different approaches to work experience, but in the past few years there have been a number of detailed research programmes into the provision of work experience and the appropriate strategies and materials.

The Schools' Council's Schools and Industry Project (SCIP) has covered work experience as part of its programme, and three LEAs – Sheffield, Strathclyde and ILEA – were each pilot projects for a joint EEC/DES/LEA examination of *Transition from School to Working Life*. Lasting for four years on average, these schemes resulted in detailed information about transition and stimulated further research into areas of the curriculum, materials, school/industry contact, record keeping and reporting, and liaison between agencies. In Sheffield the following results are evidence of what can be achieved:

– Changes in the curriculum in schools involved, including the development of a mode 3 CSE 'Understanding commerce and industry' course in one of the schools, of which work experience was an integral part.
– The provision of work experience for *all* fourth-year pupils.
– Awareness of the need to change some of the systems of transition rather than simply to adapt school–leavers to the system.
– The development of a wide range of learning materials including:
  ● a 29–page work experience booklet
  ● a guide and diary for school–leavers
  ● a handbook on what to do with spare time, listing leisure and recreational, cultural, sporting and voluntary groups in Sheffield
  ● slide/tape packs
  ● teachers' guides and worksheets.

There is now enough information available about the needs of school leavers – and particularly the 40% of lower achievers who figured in the Sheffield project – and there are enough models to consider, for schools and local authorities to improve transition and to derive the maximum benefit from work experience schemes.

CRAC have produced a *Student's Workbook* and *Teacher's Handbook on Work Experience* and the Schools' Council have produced a booklet entitled *Work Experience in the School Curriculum*. Together, these books will help you and your students to prepare fully, to structure and record observations made during the placement, and to make the experience one of the most positive learning experiences which they are likely to have outside of an integrated school/industry course, which is precisely what work experience ought to become.

iii **Things**

iii(a) **Audio-visual aids**
Films
Filmstrips
Photos
Slides
Overhead transparencies
Television
Radio
Video cassettes
Video cameras
Tapes
Tape recorders

iii(b) **Printed materials**
Books
Magazines
Handbooks
Compendiums
Prospectuses
Alternative prospectuses
Life skills programmes
Games/case studies/simulations
etc

iii(c) **Information technology and computer aids**
Prestel
'DOORS'
Computajob (COMJOB)
Advanced Computajob
(ADVCOM)
JKI
CASCAID
JIIG-CAL
Careers software packs

iii(d) **Interest and knowledge guides**
JKI (Job Knowledge Index)
OCL (Occupational Check List)
Interest Blanks (Rothwell Miller)
APU blanks

iii(a) **Audio-visual aids**
Despite the proliferation of visual and audio aids during the last two decades there is still a reluctance on the part of many teachers to make

them a regular part of their teaching and learning resources. There are two major reasons – other than lack of money – for this failure to innovate: one is organisational and the other is a problem of discrimination.

Organisational problems: A lot of time and effort has to be put into examining the catalogues, schools' television programmes, *Radio* and *TV Times* and freely distributed material in order to assess its suitability, and arranging bookings, reservations, and recordings. Teachers are prepared to do this, and many schools now have the assistance of audio-visual technicians on staff, but the problems arise in finding suitable accommodation and ensuring that the equipment is available at the appropriate time. The result is often that those departments who are fortunate enough to have equipment sited in or near their rooms and who have adequate blackout, sockets and screens have tended to use these aids more frequently than those less blessed. When the practical problems of using an aid outweigh the advantages – especially in view of the preparatory effort – then printed material will continue to replace it.

Organisational solutions: The onus lies on the teacher in charge of careers education to see that the careers teaching areas are suitably equipped with blackout, sockets and screens and that tape recorders, slide and film projectors, and overhead projectors are either sited in the department or readily accessible. The department ought to have its own video cassette recorder and access to a video camera. Agreed access at certain times to a compatible computer for use of careers programs would be an advantage. Within the next five years there is a case for a computer solely for the use of the careers department, and sited in the careers library. What you have to do is demonstrate your need for this hardware within your programme, and use existing hardware regularly until the technician gets tired of carrying it back and forth, and the other departments complain that it is never available because careers is always using it. That is how change occurs in the average school; theory, supported by good practice.

Problems of discrimination: Teachers tend to work to fairly narrowly – defined syllabi, particularly in the fourth and fifth years where these are largely dictated by examination boards. Finding films, film strips and television programmes which exactly match the requirements of the syllabus can be difficult. Because of the impact of visual material, teachers may be concerned that material might act more as a distractor than a reinforcement. The result is that far more audio-visual material is used with junior forms, and with non–exam classes. In careers, health, personal and social education this problem doesn't exist. There is a plethora of material designed to meet specific elements of personal, social and vocational development, and in some cases programmes are virtually designed around available material. If you are going to have a problem, it ought to be one of selection due to oversupply, rather than shortage.

Films There is a wide range of 16mm sound films, either free or available for a small charge, and on a short loan basis. They tend to fit into one of the following categories:

1 General introductions to broad occupational areas

eg – engineering
– women in engineering
– a career in banking/accountancy/insurance etc

2 Information produced by individual firms/services

eg – 'A career with . . .'
– the RAF/army/navy
– British Telecom
– UKAE
– British Aerospace
– The Civil Service etc

3 Information about training opportunities

eg – sponsorship
– YTS
– apprenticeship schemes

4 General introductions to further and higher education

eg – 'What are they doing at college?'
– life at university
– the colleges and institutes of higher education
– 'First days'
– 'What use is a degree?' etc

5 Information from individual institutions

eg – individual university film/video prospectuses (Sussex, Leeds, Newcastle, UMIST, Warwick etc)

6 Life skills related films (often sponsored by firms)

eg – how to prepare for an interview
– budgeting and finance
– decision–making
– exams and revision/study and learning techniques
– personal/social/health topics

Availability   The two most comprehensive sources of information about films available for your use are the Central Film Library catalogue and the COIC catalogue. The industrial training boards, professional bodies and institutions of higher education are likely to send you annual reminders of the films, booklets and video tapes on offer and CRAC and other educational software producers will supply their own catalogues. Careers Consultants have compiled a *Handbook of Free Careers Information in the UK* (1978) which you will find useful. If you have any difficulty tracking down any of these sources, contact your local careers office.

Use   There are three ways in which films are normally used: to generate a basic awareness and understanding of a particular occupation, educational or training opportunity; to stimulate discussion or personal research; and to make specific teaching or instructional points. All films, radio and television programmes have the disadvantages of including a number of distracting stimuli, and of presenting a once-and-for-all exposition unless you are willing and able to give repeat performances to the same group. It is important therefore to isolate the aspects of a film you think are important for the group, prepare them for the film in advance so that they have some idea of what to look for, and reinforce the salient points by linking them to the work which you do next – whether it takes the form of discussion, brainstorming, adding the relevant information to their personal work files, undertaking follow–up research, or – in the case of skills training – practising the techniques demonstrated in the film.

John Cleese – former teacher and current superstar of television, films, and instructional and educational films and video cassettes – recently suggested in the *Times Educational Supplement* that five teaching points was the maximum number you could hope to emphasise in a film, and still expect people to recall them. Working on this basis, and with careful preparation and follow-up, you will not only gain the maximum benefit from films, but also be helping your students to develop a systematic approach towards the use of visual material as a learning resource, rather than merely as a source of passive entertainment.

Film strips, slides, photos   These visual – and, when combined with taped commentaries, audio-visual – aids can be used for exactly the same purpose as films, and have the following advantages:
- they are relatively cheap to purchase for regular and convenient use
- they can be used in a discriminating way: certain frames or slides can be selected for particular study, and others discarded altogether
- it is easier to proceed at a pace dictated by the needs and ability of the group.
- students can use specially–prepared packs themselves, in the study carrells provided in the careers room/library, using portable cassettes and headphones and personal viewers.

The disadvantages tend to be that many commentaries are monotone, boring and unsuited to certain groups. If this is the case, then discard the commentary and either tape or give your own – or, better still, let a group of students prepare their own using a variety of voices.

The same sources given for films will provide filmstrips and tapes, and a number of educational publishers like CRAC/Hobsons Press produce special packs related to careers objectives.

Photos are most often used as a stimulus or as background information in displays, and it is a good idea to take a good 35mm camera on visits and when following up work experience placements. The camera club at school will develop and enlarge them for you, and they can feature in your work experience preparation displays.

Radio and tapes   Students are now conditioned to the visual stimulus to such an extent that the use of radio programmes or tape recordings of more than five minutes' duration is likely to result in rapid deterioration in interest, concentration and recall. The only exceptions are likely to be individual students or very small groups given a series of tasks based on a recording, and I am convinced that this is the best way to proceed. Alternatively, a lengthy recording can be interrupted at appropriate intervals to discuss or make notes on the points raised so far. Of greater potential is the use of the *tape recorder* as an active learning resource.

The use of tape–recorded interviews with family, friends and people met on visits and work experience placements, is one way in which the students can bring these external environments and related attitudes into the classroom for examination. The skills involved in preparing for these interviews, undertaking them and editing and presenting the information gained, are in themselves valuable social and learning skills.

Video cassettes and video cameras   The most potent and flexible teaching aid in careers education is most definitely the combined resource of the video camera and recorder. These can be used in the following ways:

The video recorder:
- to cover all of the objectives available with a film; awareness, information and skill instruction, with the added benefits of 'pause' and 'freeze' control, instant replay and editing by use of fast forward control. More selective use, and better reinforcement of salient points, becomes possible.
- to record any television programmes which have been released from copyright for schools, and to use them when it is appropriate and convenient to do so.
- to play back your own, and the students' own, recordings.
- to play the commercially–produced cassettes which are rapidly replacing 16mm films.

Using the video camera:
- to make our own specific programmes eg: interviewing; induction to FE or the sixth form; sixth form video prospectus; work experience preparation; YTS; attitudes to work and leisure; opportunities in the local community – work, leisure, voluntary service; introducing the careers service (in collaboration with your careers officer or local careers workshop).
- to enable students to collaborate in the making of the above programmes.
- to record 'mock interview' sessions for analysis.
- for students to make their own 'video self-presentation' or 'video application' as a means of developing self-confidence and self-awareness, and as a preparation for interviews.
- to record role plays and case studies for analysis and discussion.
- to record visiting speakers who may not be able to address all of the appropriate groups.

The systems available are now exceptionally easy to use – virtually teacher–proof – and, in the case of the cameras, the students will soon show you how to use them effectively. This year some sixth form students helped to produce a sixth form video prospectus for the author, and a particularly enthusiastic group of fourteen–year–olds – of varied academic ability – produced a school video prospectus for the incoming first year students and their parents, and followed the school's page in the local paper through from sorting the articles out to the final compositing stage at the paper's offices. The latter project has provided a fascinating insight into the work of a newspaper sub-editor and editor, and will be used not only by the careers department, but also in the English department and on the TVEI 'Communications' course. All of the editing was done by these students and they used the school's, and their own, computers to produce the accompanying graphics.

Once you begin to use a video camera, the only problems you are likely to face are to do with becoming obsessed with it. Trying to produce a perfect finished product may be laudable – and on occasions will be advantageous, especially when showing a film to large groups for example at parents' evenings – but don't forget its potential for recording things as they happen, unscripted and unrehearsed. Once it becomes a regular tool in the hands of the students you will really begin to reap the benefits. Naturally, you will have to explore how far you can use it for group or individual self–analysis at first, but providing you follow the same guidelines of tact and sensitivity which you would use in a normal role play or self–awareness session, and allow the students to become used to it first, there is no reason why it shouldn't become a learning aid which they enjoy using far more than the tape recorder with its 'disembodied' mirror of their voices.

Here are a few suggestions on how to introduce the video camera as an aid:
1 Begin by showing commercial cassettes as part of the careers programme.
2 Introduce some structured topics which you or a group of students have made.
3 Introduce the camera; show them how to operate it.
4 Let them take it in turns to film you, and each other, and play back their efforts.
5 Set up a role play – a deliberately bad interview for example – or a case study, and allow some of the students to record it. Play it back for discussion, ensuring that any analysis or discussion is limited to the questions raised, or the behaviour of the characters being played, and *not* of the students playing the parts.
6 After regular use as in 5 above it should be possible to move on to analysis of straight interviews, and use for self–presentations, without any more embarrassment or sense of threat than that which would have existed 'doing it in front of the class' and almost certainly with more personal gain for the students involved.

General hints
– never try to 'catch them unawares'; always be honest about what you are

doing and why, and how you intend to use it.

– never show a group or individual on cassette to another group or person, without the foreknowledge and permission of those on the recording.

– always wipe clean immediately anything which you have agreed not to show anybody other than the participants.

We all have the slightly uneasy feeling of the American Indians that someone who possesses a photo or a moving picture of us somehow has power over us. It may just be a fear that we might be held up to ridicule – consciously or accidentally – but it is a real fear, and a real danger when dealing with young people. Use the camera tactfully, honestly and with a clear purpose, and it will become an excellent teaching and learning aid.

Overhead projectors   There are a number of commercial packs on the market which use a series of overhead transparencies for careers education topics. The CRAC *Computajob* and *Advanced Computajob* kits use acetate overlays onto a numbered grid in order to relate factors in job choice to specific occupations. They can be used for group or class discussion or for individual research without needing to use an overhead projector, simply by laying them on top of a white carbon cartridge paper.

You can also produce your own transparencies for outlining decision–making strategies, option choices, levels of entry, job families, leavers' destinations, occupational structures, economic statistics. . . . Really the list is endless. The advantage is of course that you don't have to keep writing on the board, or handing out duplicated sheets to group after group and year after year. The only disadvantage is that you have to have an OHP and screen in the room in which you are teaching. If you can't justify that, there isn't much hope for a video recorder and camera!

iii(b) **Printed materials**

The list of printed materials available for careers education and information is given at the beginning of this section. It would take a book several times the length of this one simply to review them. In Appendix 3 you will find a list of major publishers of careers materials. The best materials always include details on how to use them, and you can always refer to the section of methods in this book. Send for the free catalogues and go to your nearest careers resource centre – listed in the training section – and view before you buy. If there is a careers workshop group in your area ask for their advice on which material is suitable and effective with the relevant groups. There really is so much available now that you must find out all you can about it first, and choose carefully. Buy in haste and repent at leisure! By all means begin to produce your own worksheets and games, but don't be tempted to break copyright. Apart from impoverishing the poor authors – many of them teachers like you – it does make it harder for the publishers to produce more material for your use, and it can be a costly mistake. It's worth noting that *some* of the lifeskills and careers materials can seem expensive for a single pack or copy but these then release you from copyright, and allow you to make multiple copies of the materials.

Storing workcards and worksheets can be a problem. There are four main answers to this problem: multi–drawer filing cabinets; box files; trays on wall racks or shelves; envelopes suspended from racks or within standing cabinets. Have a look at systems used in the school, ask for the educational furniture catalogue, ask the commercial department for their office supplies catalogue, and you should have plenty to choose from to suit your needs.

iii(c) **Information technology and computer aids**

At the moment we are on the threshold of an information technology revolution in education, but already there are applications in careers education and guidance which give us an indication of how it might develop. There are four basic categories of use:

1 **Databases** These are straightforward banks of information which students and their advisers can use in the same way that they would have used a compendium in the past, but with greater ease and flexibility. The following examples are already available:

– **Prestel** COIC is an information–provider to the British Telecom system. The COIC pages provide details of over 300 occupations which can be accessed by use of an alphabetical index, by 10 interest categories such as 'scientific', 'caring', or 'practical', or by school subject. A service of news items is also provided for careers and employment advisers.

– **DOORS** is another computerized system which is undergoing trials for COIC at present. It is intended to hold data on 800–1,000 different occupations. When it becomes available to the general user it will be possible to search for occupations according to a whole range of requirements, for example:
  – O–level entry
  – regular hours
  – of a scientific nature
  – low level of mobility required
  – average salary over £7,000
  – regular vacancies

Problems of storage and retrieval of careers information will be reduced dramatically, and ease of updating will follow from central programming by COIC or a trained user at a local careers office or job centre.

At present these systems tend to be located in central offices like the careers office, but any school with televisions modified to accept Prestel can use the system like any subscriber, and there is no reason why a system like DOORS couldn't be made available in the same way. There is no reason why they should not be available to the school's careers department where they could be used as a complementary or supplementary database to Signposts, and an ideal tool for careers education and individual guidance, rather than as a replacement for the placement role of the careers service.

2 Quizzes and games   The presentation of information in quiz form, and of decision–making strategies in the form of a game. The latter method has not yet been reflected in software but will be sure to shortly.

- **Job Knowledge Index (JKI)**   Devised in printed form by M J Kirton and published by Heinemann and COIC, this system is now being pilot tested as a computer program for the RML 380Z. Aimed at students who are expected to gain good O–level results and beyond, it provides a battery of questions about a particular career. Students are required to answer 'true', 'false' or 'don't know' to each question, and then check their answers with the correct responses. In this way they will be able to test their knowledge of an occupational area and acquire a better understanding of it through active participation. The printed version was intended primarily for use in a group session with an adviser trained in the use of the indices by the Occupational Research Centre. The computerised version is going to be more appropriate to individual research, unless you happen to have a surfeit of computers for careers use.

3 Combined database/interest guide/job quiz   All sorts of combinations are possible, but the computerised version of the CRAC *Computajob* and *Advanced Computajob* packs is a representative example.

- **Basic careers kit COMJOB:** aimed at 13 + students, it explores occupations not requiring formal entry qualifications and can be used flexibly under the headings:
  OPTION – relating careers to subject choice
  INTRST – an occupational interest guide
  JOBQUZ – a test of occupational knowledge.
- **Advcom kit:** aimed at the 14–17–year–old, it is really a straight computerised version of *Advanced Computajob*, as described in the section on OHPs.
- **Univch kit:** aimed at 15 + students contemplating higher education, it is primarily a database of information about the geographical and environmental aspects of universities.

4 Computer–assisted guidance   This category really belongs in the section of this book reserved for careers guidance systems, but all of the examples in general use are equally tools for education and for guidance. *A detailed analysis of each appears in the guidance section* but briefly the two major systems are:

- **CASCAID**   Developed by the Leicestershire Careers Service, the letters stand for Careers Advisory Service Computer Aid. Aimed at occupations requiring three or more O–levels – and particularly at the A–level student – it matches a student's self–concept in relation to work at that moment in time to a job bank of over 400 careers. In addition to the student's responses regarding occupational activities and working environments, physical disabilities, aversions, and stated career intentions, it takes into account current and estimated examination results. It is available for use only by trained careers officers, and is normally operated in 'batch mode', which means that a careers officer briefs a group of students in the purpose of the exercise and the method of filling in the questionnaire, collects the completed forms at a later date, codes them for processing through the computer and then books an individual interview with each student to discuss the printout in relation to the student's original responses. A CASCAID HE is available for students in higher education.

– **JIIG–CAL**   Developed as two separate systems – one by the business studies department at Edinburgh University and the other by the educational computer centre of the London Borough of Havering – and the letters stand for Job Ideas and Information Generator – Computer Assisted Learning. The title accurately describes the purpose of the system and it is intended to be used with groups of students across the whole ability range from the fourth year onwards. Trained careers officers or careers teachers are able to use the system. Used within the larger framework of a careers programme it guides students through the process of considering their occupational interests, expanding their awareness of occupational factors, ordering their priorities and examining the 20 best job matches produced on their personal computer printout. The initial system was made available only on 'batch mode', requires at least four sessions, and group and individual discussions with the trained operators are essential.

Both CASCAID and JIIG–CAL are relatively expensive in terms of manpower, but offer an excellent opportunity for the exercise of self–awareness, opportunity awareness and decision–making skills, and can provide common ground and a useful starting point for careers guidance interviews during the fifth year or sixth year.

Do–it–yourself computer programs   Once you have convinced the holders of the privy purse that you need and will make good use of a computer in the careers office/room/library, and have made sure that it is compatible with the majority of commercial programs, why not design your own programs? Or better still, explain your problem and persuade some of the experienced programmers among the students to come up with a solution. In the appendix you will find such a program. Designed to run on the Commodore PET it guides a student through the relevant stages of a 'Job search' or a 'Higher education search' and indicates, on a diagram of the careers library represented in this book, where the appropriate information can be found. This program was produced by a twelve–year–old student, armed only with the flow chart listed in the appendix.

iii(d) Interest and knowledge guides

There is an increasingly wide range of questionnaires, guides and tests designed to achieve one or more of the following objectives:

- a test of intelligence
- a test of aptitude
- a test of personality
- a test of achievement
- a test of occupational interests
- a test of personal values and interests.

Some of these tests, and tests disguised as questionnaires, are intended to give a more objective assessment of a student's ability, potential, personality and interests than that which is available through the normal school system of assessment and reports. Where this is the case, these tests are for use in a guidance context, and are examined in Part 4 of this book. Those guides which are designed to give the student a better awareness of his interests, values and preferences, and to test or improve his understanding of occupational roles, are primarily educational, but provide a good basis for guidance. *JKIs*, *Computajob* and *Advanced Computajob* fall into this latter category, whilst A D Crowley's *Occupational Check List* (OCL) stands firmly in the centre; an excellent guidance tool, and of increasing value as an exercise in self–awareness as students become more mature.

Whichever category of questionnaire you happen to be using, always remember that a response by the student indicating an occupational interest does not necessarily mean that they have good knowledge of that occupation. Also, distinguish between those tests which are looking for inherent aptitudes, interests or personality traits and those which draw upon the student's self–concept. It is very easy when resources are limited to assume that the student's conscious responses are an accurate reflection of the person they are, or of the person they wish to become. The fact that the two are not synonymous helps to explain why careers education needs to proceed in tandem with guidance.

D Pulling it all together

A careers education programme

So far we have considered the objectives of careers education, how it might be organised, and the methods and resources available. Here, at last, is a sample programme. No self–respecting handbook would be caught without one. It is, however, only an example of how you might pull together the various strands to produce a coherent teaching and learning strategy. If you have just landed – or been landed with – the job of introducing or developing a careers education programme, this model is as good as any to set you thinking, but you will have to go through the process of deciding what *your* students need, what is possible *now*, and where *you* want the programme to be in several years' time.

It was explained earlier in this book that we have proceeded on the basis of selecting those objectives which are common needs, and which relate directly to the development of an occupational self–concept, and the skills needed for successful transition. In other words, we are only concerned here with the particular objectives of careers education.

The programme therefore represents a careers 'Addition' approach which can be used equally to consider what elements need to be developed, and at what stages, in a school which wishes to 'infuse' careers education throughout the curriculum.

To compromise between the feeling that one ought to provide some guidelines, but that it is important for you to do your own information–seeking and decision–making, you will find suggested methods and resources for the third and sixth years only.

Two publications which will prove invaluable throughout the programme in providing examples of simulations, role plays, games, exercises, and other active learning methods are *Exercises in Personal and Careers Development* by Barrie Hopson and Patricia Hough (CRAC) and *Life Skills Teaching* packs 1 and 2, by Barrie Hopson and Mike Scally (McGraw Hill).

Finally, because careers is not an examined subject there is a tendency to forget to evaluate how far you have achieved your objective. Granted that in some cases the benefits will only emerge well into the future, many of the objectives are to do with skills or with transition. Evaluation is important, and because there are no exams you can make it more enjoyable. In any case, students expect you to find out how well they have understood and assimilated information and developed skills, and it is a reinforcement which is a healthy part of the learning process. Keep the results to yourself by all means, make it a corporate activity by pyramiding, but evaluate each section as an aid to refining and improving your programme.

Abbreviations of objectives used in the programme

O/A	Opportunity awareness
S/A	Self awareness
DM	Decision making
TR	Transition (including coping/survival skills)
CM	Communication skills
STL	Study and learning skills
INF	Information skills
SS	Social skills.

The objectives listed alongside each section of the programme on the following pages are – when in bold – prime objectives which one would consciously seek to meet. The other objectives are secondary ones which are likely to be achieved, but which should only be consciously pursued when they can be linked with, and complement, the prime objectives. Always set specific goals and aim to meet those first, before pursuing subsidiary goals.

A sample careers education programme

Third year

(A file – 'My careers file' – issued, to be built up and kept by the students until they leave and take it with them.)

Objective	Theme		Methods/resources
Term 1			
TR; O/A	**Introducing the programme** (Is there life after school? Will I be ready?) How we spend our time How adults spend their time		Brainstorm/talk Video – past students Pyramiding. Lists. TV. Questionnaires. Parents.
O/A INF	**Occupations?**		
	Paid work	– Full–time – Part–time – Temporary – 'Black economy'	Newspapers Magazines Questionnaires Brainstorms/Pyramids 'Heroes and heroines' Role play
	Unpaid work	– Housework – child rearing – 'Voluntary work' – (social, civic, political)	Parents, and other visiting adults as examples, video Taped interviews. TV/films.
	Training	– Full–time – Part–time – YTS	Ex–students now in training. – Video
	Education	– Full–time grant/no grant – Part–time	– Ex–students now in FE
	Leisure	– Physical – Artistic/creative – Intellectual etc	The students themselves, members of staff with hobbies/interests. TV. Video Parents–questionnaires
	Evaluation and link		
S/A	**Abilities; interests; values** Who am I?		
	Physical characteristics Health		The student/parents.
	Interests/activities		The student. *Occupational interest blanks*
	Abilities		The student/friends/parents. (Mirrors)
	Values		The student. Pyramids. Questionnaires. *Your choice at 13+* PIG

This information forms the beginning of each student's personal profile.

Objective	Theme	Methods/resources

Term 2

O/A S/A **Subject choice**
DM
a Why choose?   *Your Choice at 13+*
– Reasons for the existing   TV/video
  curriculum   Director of studies
– Public examinations, levels
  and links
– Options open to you
– Vocational and personal
  implications of choices
– Factors in choice – ability
                    – interest
                    – motivation
                    – vocational
                    – sex stereo-   GIST materials
                      types   *Male and female*

INF   – Sources of information:
             uses and limitations of
                                        – tutor
                                        – subject teachers
                                        – heads of department
                                        – deputy heads
                                        – parents
                                        – friends
                                        – careers teacher
                                        – careers library
                                        – careers officer
                                        – careers convention

b Job and training families   *Work Experience Projects*
                                        Job Quiz 1: Job Knowledge
                                        COIC/CLCI *Index*
                                        MSC YTS Indexes
                                        Careers library
                                        TV/video. Films

c Levels of entry   As above

d Occupational use of option   *Your Choice at 13+*
   subjects   *Basic Careers*
                                        Heads of Department
                                        Hopson and Hough

e 'Lifestyle' plan 1

Objective	Theme	Methods/resources
Term 3		
DM	**Guided choice**	*Your Choice at 13+* *Basic Careers* *Job Quiz 2* Careers/subject staff
SS CM S/A DM	**Group work** to build social skills and to reinforce and evaluate work done so far. Including:	Ice breakers Trust games Role plays Hopson and Scally Hopson and Hough
	Transition to fourth year Preparing a personal contract for their own profiles: 'Next year I will . . .'	The students; their profiles. The careers teacher.

Fourth year

Objective	Theme	Methods/resources

Term 1

O/A INF SS TR	**Unpaid occupations research** The responsibilities and rewards of different roles: – student – friend – citizen – homemaker – spouse – parent – leisurite	2
O/A INF SS TR S/A	**Paid occupations research** A more detailed examination of paid occupations – using *JIIG-CAL* to consider: 1 – job levels 2 – interests 3 – analysis of 1 and 2 4 – job aspects	
O/A **INF** TR STL	**A Personal Project** To investigate job areas revealed by JIIG-CAL, in the careers library, using *SPEED COP** headings as a guide. *See 'Hopson and Hough' (CRAC): S Surroundings P Prospects E Entry and training E Effects D Descriptions C Conditions O Organisation P People	

Term 2

O/A
S/A
	'Lifestyle' plan 2
	Understanding industry
	a Student's impressions of
	    industry
	b Why work?
	c Basic sectors – primary
	                  – secondary
	                  – tertiary
	d Organisations
	    The structure of – firms
	                     – companies
	    'Small is beautiful?'
	    – Self employment	

O/A **TR**	**Changing patterns of** **employment** 'Coping with change'	

Objective	Theme	Methods/resources
DM CM SS INF **TR** O/A	**Business games** Simulations, case studies, games and role plays, to reinforce a–d	

Term 3

	Work experience	

TR
INF
CM
SS
DM
O/A
S/A
	a Preparation for work
	experience placements, covering:
	– purpose
	– organisation
	– availability
	– choice
	– expectations
	– tasks – observing
	     – interviewing
	     – recording
	     (use of the log book)
	     – reporting back	

	b Placement	
TR O/A **CM** SS	**c Reporting back** Sharing of experiences using log books, questionnaires, taped interviews, discussion, brainstorms etc. Link with previous *SPEEDCOP* exercise.	
TR	**Transition to fifth year** Work experience log added to personal career file, and a new contract arrived at for next year.	

Fifth year

Objective	Theme	Methods/resources

Term 1

O/A;
TR
Timetable of year decision points
– careers interviews
– mocks and exam estimates
– dates for applications to:
  – apprenticeship
  – employment
  – YTS
  – FE/sixth form
  – official 'leaving dates'

DM
Deciding – a decision–making strategy

INF
Sources of information revised (with special reference to the careers interview)

S/A
Seven–point self assessment
1 Educational achievement and potential
2 Strongest abilities
3 Personal qualities
4 Physical characteristics and health
5 Domestic circumstances affecting choice
6 Interests and activities
7 Occupational interests or intentions

O/A
16+ choice: the alternatives
Current availability and nature of:
– Paid employment, with or without training
– YTS
– Further education – tertiary/ FE/sixth form/ sixth form college
– Alternatives during unemployment
– Sources of help

TR
Applications

TR
CM
Methods of application
Making the most of a form
My own *curriculum vitae*
My personal record

Objective	Theme	Methods/resources
Term 2		
TR/CM	**Interview skills** – using information gained on work experience plus inputs from ex–students and employers	
TR	**Budgeting** Methods of pay and deductions Social security; grants Why budget? How to budget Banking services	
STL	**Preparing for exams** Exam and revision techniques	
TR	**Easter leavers' check list and action pack**	
Term 3		
	During this term many schools allow their students to take study leave after a certain time. Levels of concentration in non–academic subjects are also noticeably – and understandably – low. The limited time available is certainly worth spending as indicated, and with relaxed individual guidance as required.	
TR	**Transition to further education** Using a further education SPEEDCOP (See *Experiments in Personal and Career Development*, Hopson and Hough)	
TR DM	**Leaving check list and action pack** (What to do if, and when, and how. Sources of help. How to use your careers file to help you. Keeping us informed.)	

Sixth year

(This programme makes two assumptions: firstly, that there are complementary general/liberal studies and moral/RE programmes which cover the political, cultural, economic, moral and social issues in the same way that these were assumed to be part of the curriculum for years three to five; and secondly, that wherever possible the careers education and guidance of students on one–year courses is an integral part of their course, linking the periods of pre–vocational learning and work experience with the work covered in the first three years of the course. Elements that would be common to both A–level and pre–vocational students are indicated by an asterisk, but in the interests of building their confidence, self–esteem, sense of purpose, and group as well as individual commitment, one–year students and their needs should be regarded as special, particular, and be consciously met from within their own course.)

Objectives

Term 1	Theme	Methods/resources
TR Induction	**Working the system*** Study and learning techniques Continuous assessment Tutorials Why am I here?	Individual and group exercises on reading/notemaking/memory/researching skills/Seventh year and ex–students. Staff, video.
O/A	**Outline programme** and* decision points Destinations	OHP. Talk
INF	**Sources of information*** Careers officer Careers library specific information	OHP. Career officer Careers library Video of student working through a 'search'
O/A	**Future shock?*** Changing patterns of employment and of leisure. Coping with change.	Group discussions, Pyramids. OHP Talks, based on *Future Shock* *Leisure Shock* *The Collapse of Work* The Warwick study 'Redundant', 'retired' adults
S/A **DM** O/A SS	Values and lifestyles*	Games: Survivors' *Deciding* Exercises – *Experiments in Personal and Career Development*, Hopson and Hough; *Life Skills Teaching*, Hopson and Scally.

111

Objective	Theme	Methods/resources
S/A O/A	**Male and female*** The implications – vocational/ personal – of sex stereotyping	*Male and Female* *Women at Work* GIST Film: *Jobs for the Girls* *Experiments in Personal and Career Development* *Life Skills Teaching* The students
S/A O/A	**'Lifestyle' plan 3*** Students draw up 'ideal' and 'possible' life plan	
O/A D/M S/A	**Routes; 17+ Choice*** Considering the alternatives and the routes by which they can be reached. Including: A Year Off?	*Your Choice at 17+; Decide for Yourself Routes.* Individual exercises. OHPs
O/A	**Advanced Computajob** Use of *Advcom* to explore paid occupations according to students' own criteria	*Time to Spare Advcom* OHP Demonstration Use by students
O/A; S/A	**CASCAID** A batch presentation of CASCAID for those students who wish to take up the opportunity	CASCAID Careers officer Follow up interviews

---

Term 2

O/A	**Occupational Information*** A series of films; videos; visiting employers/representatives of employers. Training officers; and visits to places of employment	Employers and training officers Films. Talks Visits Discussions
	plus **Academic 'Vocational' information** Lectures; talks; visits; films; to indicate vocational implications of higher education subject choices NB Both of the above themes will occur throughout the course and depend as much on the availability of speakers/films/open days, as on optimum timing.	Higher education Lecturers and films etc Visits
O/A	**'Job search'**	

Objective	Theme	Methods/resources
INF	An introduction to the use of JKIs. Followed by use of JKIs in examining occupations suggested by the individual CASCAID printouts. Leading onto personal research in the careers library	JKIs. Demonstration. Careers Library. 'Job search' computer program
O/A **INF**	**Sponsorship; traineeship; studentship** An examination of the nature of these options. Benefits and limitations. Where to find out about them. When and how to apply.	*Your Choice at 17+* *The Sponsorship Programme*[†] Sponsorships and supplementary awards. *Changing Tracks*[††]

[†] = CRAC/COIC film strip.
[††] = CRAC/British Leyland film.

Term 3

O/A	**Introduction to further and higher education choice** Why bother? **Qualifications** Foundation Higher diplomas and certificates Professional diplomas/certificates Diplomas of higher education Degrees – BA, BSc, BHum, BEd, MA, etc Postgraduate qualifications	*Your choice at 17+*. *On from A–levels. What use is a degree? The Degree Choice Programme* COIC filmstrip Compendiums Handbooks *What Do Graduates Do?* etc
	Courses Nature (Academic/vocational) Duration. Entry requirements Sandwich and integrated Enhanced	Careers library Visiting speakers HE forum: ex-students *Degree Offers* Prospectuses
	Institutions Colleges of FE Polytechnics Universities Colleges/institutes of HEd Professional institutes	*The New Colleges of Higher Education. CRAC The Polytechnics — Staff and Students Talking.* COIC University and polytechnic video prospectuses Open days/visits
	Methods of application Form; letter; interview UCCA Central clearing houses	Sample forms/OHPs *How to apply to University* UCCA *Grants to students: A Brief Guide.* DES
	Can I afford it? Fees. Grants. Accommodation	'How to Covenant' Scholarships and local awards

Objective	Theme	Methods/resources
O/A **INF** TR	**Higher education search** Individual research in the careers library and writing for information	Careers library Higher education search computer program ECCTIS
O/A INF	**Work experience placement** For A–level students this is likely to be arranged for holiday periods, or during regular 'study time' afternoons. It is more likely to be linked to areas of aspiration, and to have a 'tasting' or 'information' motive.	Careers officer Project Trident Employers
DM **INF** **O/A**	**Holiday action plan** Deciding what steps to take during the holiday in pursuit of information to help their own job, higher education, or 'time out' plans. All information and ideas entered in personal careers file and record as in previous years.	Individual guidance from careers staff Careers library Careers officer

Seventh year

It is rare to find 'careers' timetabled in the sixth year – rare enough to find it at all in the sixth form – and the emphasis certainly moves towards individual guidance as students begin to pursue their own plans and applications. The appropriate decision points are listed in the guidance calendar which follows shortly, but there are the following common elements which should be covered, and for which some form of timetable provision should be made:

Objective	Theme	Methods/resources
CM/TR INF **S/A** CM	**Applications and forms reviewed*** Personal record and cv updated*	Blanks; examples; exercises
CM	**Interview techniques*** (Including the provision of mock interviews by staff, prior to actual interviews)	*The Interview Programme* CRAC/Midland Bank *Going for an Interview* COIC/DITB Role plays
DM	**Deadlines and 'backups'*** A reminder about closing dates and the need for contingency plans	Careers staff/officer
TR	**Budgeting and finance*** Reminders about grants; pay; social security; banking services. Covenanting	DES and LEA pamphlets; Bank 'student officers'; Comparing bank student offers Blank forms
	Student start To prepare potential students for transition to higher education	*First Days* film Barclays Bank *Student Hindsight* Ex–students forum
	Employment start* Review their work experience; discuss what they need to be aware of during the first month Self–employment reviewed Advanced training schemes	Discussion–pyramid Ex–students Employers View *Beginners*, a CYEE/ Leicestershire film; and think of making your own video using ex–students
	What if?* Coping strategies for: – unemployment – grades too low – a change of mind	Careers officer FEIS briefing DM revised and sources of help
	Clearing procedure and action pack Careers file to keep and . . . use?	

PART 4

Careers guidance

Definition

guide (gid)n 1   *One who shows the way*

counsel 1 n   Deliberation or debate (take c, *think or talk over what is to be done*, often together with advice).

Source: *The New Oxford Illustrated Dictionary*

A Aims and objectives

There are many models of guidance and definitions of counselling, but these dictionary definitions are an accurate description of good practice.

In Part 3, the point was made that careers education and guidance have the same aim of developing vocational maturity, and that guidance is essentially an educative process. The only real difference between them is the method by which they function. Careers education uses 'lesson' time to meet *common* needs and to give students opportunities to explore their own *particular* needs. This is apparent from the sample careers education programme. General examinations of opportunities are always followed by individual research, and in the case of JIIG-CAL and CASCAID, education and guidance run firmly in tandem.

Careers guidance consists of activities – usually and preferably on a one–to–one basis – intended to meet the *particular* needs of *individual* students, and should always be an educative experience. It also has the specific intention of *helping a student to become self–directing in relation to vocational maturity*, but this is going to prove impossible if guidance is conducted in a 'careers' vacuum.

Stages of vocational maturity

In Diagram 8 (page 50) is offered a simplified model of the process of vocational maturity. For the purpose of guidance, the essential questions being asked are:

– Who do I want to be?
– How do I get there?
– How do I allow for change in me, or in the opportunities available?

It has been established that the answer to these questions depends upon:

– capacity
– inclination
– opportunity

Now it is easy to see where the objectives of careers education and guidance fit in:

Who do I want to be?	How do I get there/allow for change?	
Objectives	Objectives	
Self awareness	Decision Making	
(Capacity)	Communication	
(Inclination)	Information	**Skills**
Opportunity awareness	Transition	
(Opportunity)	Coping	

The reason we have to have a guidance system as well as a programme of education in order to meet these objectives is that the process of vocational maturation is an evolutionary one, and people have a habit of developing at different speeds. Diagram 12 (below) is a schematic presentation of several theories of vocational development. The first three stages are common to most children and are the fairly easily recognisable ones of *fantasy* ('I want to be an astronaut/ballet dancer' – no sexism intended!), *tentative* ('I might be . . .'), and *realistic* ('I hope to be a Civil Service clerical officer, or a bank clerk grade 2, but I'll apply for other things as well'). Most students are only just in the realistic stage by the time they are eligible to leave school, and for some it can take until the mid–20s before they can make a realistic choice about anything.

Diagram 12 Stages of vocational development (a traditional model)

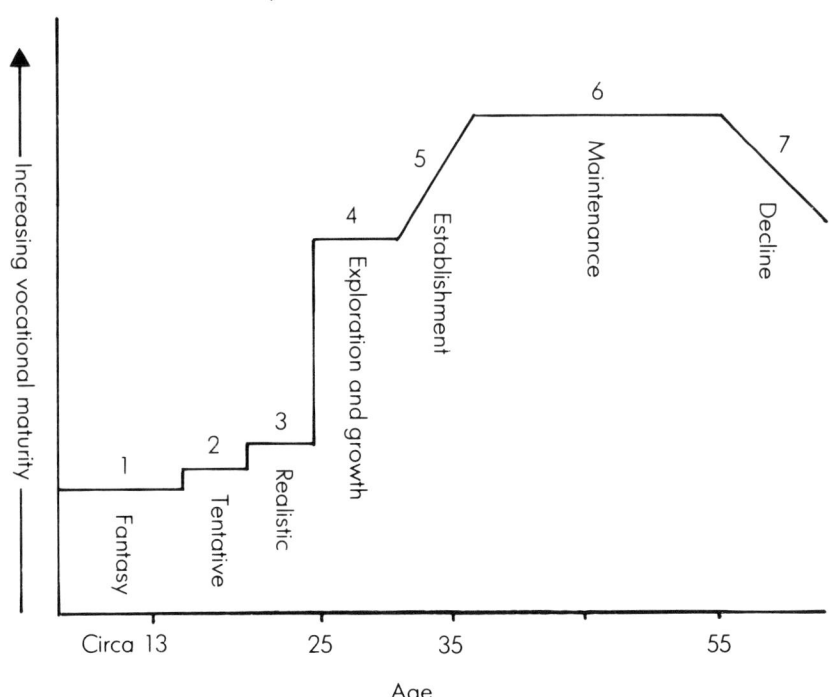

The remaining stages – from 4 to 7 – are broadly in line with the traditional pattern of career development that was outlined in Diagram 4 (page 28). There is a period of *exploration* of the suitable paid occupations and of the first one 'chosen', followed by a period of *establishment* which for the capable, ambitious and fortunate is accompanied by promotion. This is followed by a period of *maintenance* which might be by choice, or because opportunities for advancement have ceased. Finally, there is a period of *decline* as preparation is made for retirement.

Compare this with the emerging pattern of career development offered in Diagram 5 (page 29) and you will see that vocational development is a far more dynamic process in the second model, needing constant reassessment and more frequent periods of exploration and establishment. Retirement, for example, has its own period of exploration, growth and establishment. The guidance process has not only to help students through the first three stages, but also to prepare them to cope with the frequent choices and readjustments which they are going to have to make in relation to paid and unpaid occupations in the future.

Vocational maturity necessitates bringing together the personal, educational and vocational aspects of a student, and their artificial separation in the interests of 'efficiency' demands close co–operation between 'personal', 'academic', and 'vocational' counsellors, and their systems.

The following case study may help to pull together some of these points.

Michael West

Michael is in his third year at a comprehensive high school. He is the first child in the family; his brother aged 11 is in the first year and he has a ten–year–old sister at a feeder primary school. His father is a miner; his mother is a housewife and has a part–time job in the Miners' Social Club. Michael is a very talented boy. Following the third year exams he has been recommended for GCE courses in ten subjects. His subject staff believe that he has the potential to achieve 'A' grades in all of them. He is industrious but has lots of commonsense, and enjoys his free time.

Michael enjoys swimming, is a member of his local parish youth club and an enthusiastic member of the school's computer club. His abiding passion is music. He has a natural 'ear' and sings in the lower school choir, as well as playing the cornet in the Wigan Schools' Junior Brass Band.

The presenting problem

Michael has chosen all of his option subjects for the fourth year – maths, English, RE, careers and games are compulsory – and is left with a clash between music and German. Michael is good at both subjects but has not chosen French as one of his other options because that was the one subject which he did not enjoy, or perform well in. His head of music declares that he 'must' take music, and the head of modern languages says that he 'must' take German. Both teachers state that there are good cultural and vocational reasons why their subject should be taken. Michael can't make up his mind. He tells his form tutor and is referred to the head of year, and then to the head of careers. The head of careers has read Michael's school record file containing the information given above, and Michael has brought his careers file with him.

The interview

The head of careers settles Michael down by welcoming him in a relaxed manner and by apologising for the fact that the curriculum limits choices in this way. She goes on to say that she is aware of the nature of his problem but would like him to explain it himself. From the way in which he presents the problem she gets the impression that he really would like to do both subjects, would prefer to do music but feels that he ought to do German without really knowing why. She asks him the following questions, and receives the following replies.

Q : *'Why do you want to do music?'*
A: 'Because I enjoy it. I've always liked music. Now that I'm in the band and the choir I enjoy it even more. I know that it won't be any use to me for getting jobs and so on, but I want to keep it up after I leave.'

Q : *'You know that there are jobs for people who want to work with music, and take it seriously?'*
A: 'Yes. Mr Boyce (the head of music) told me about the Royal Northern College of Music, and what some of his ex–students have done. Some of the band want to go there. My dad says there's not a lot of future in it.'

Q : *'What do you think, Michael?'*
A: 'I agree. I mean it's all right for anybody who wants to make their living out of it, like Mr Boyce and Mr Lever (the peripatetic music teacher and brass band leader) but I don't want to be that serious. Playing music is all right but I think I would get bored teaching it. Anyway, there aren't many jobs are there?'

Q : *'No, you're quite right. Full time paid employment is not easy to come by, but that is true of a lot of occupations. It depends, as you say, on how serious you are, and how much of a risk you are prepared to take. What about German, Michael? Why do you want to take that?'*
A: 'Well . . . I'm good at it . . . everybody says I've got to have a language . . .'

Q : *'Everybody?'*
A: 'Well Mr Grant (the French teacher), Mrs Lees (head of modern languages), Miss Walsh (form tutor), Mr James (head of year) . . . and you did during careers.'

Q : 'Do you remember why I said that we advise everyone to try to continue studying at least one foreign language? You can check in your file if you need to, Michael.' (He doesn't need to.)

A: 'Well . . . you said that it was a bit selfish to expect everyone else to learn English. That it would make visits abroad more enjoyable – whether we were on holiday or to do with work of some kind, and that you need another language for certain jobs and courses.'

Q : 'Very good. I think I also said that for some jobs a language was essential, and for others an advantage?'

A: (Michael responds with a nod)

Q : 'Have you thought about the kinds of employment you might consider looking closely at next year, Michael? One of the job families perhaps?'

A: 'Yes. Something to do with maths or computing, or maybe with physics. Maybe engineering.'

Q : 'In that case, you'd better find out if German would be an advantage in any of those areas?'

A: (Another nod)

Q : 'And what about further courses? Have you thought about going on into the sixth form, and perhaps onto polytechnic or university?'

A: (There is a slight pause.) 'Well . . . yes. I want to go into the sixth form, and I think I want to go to university. All the teachers seem to expect me to, anyway. But I don't know if I can.'

Q : 'How do you mean Michael? All of your teachers feel that you are capable of reaching that standard.'

A: 'Well it's not that, Miss. You see my dad doesn't earn all that much, and he retires when I'm twenty. He wants me to go to university, and so does me mam, but I don't think they could afford to send me.'

Q : 'I see. And your mum and dad may still have your brother and sister to support at that stage?'

A: 'Yes, Miss. And my dad says what if they want to go to college as well?'

Q : 'Well, it's not as much of a problem as you and your dad think it is, Michael. For a start, the course fees are all paid for by Wigan, and secondly, your accommodation and money for books and living expenses are also provided, depending on how much your parents are earning at the time and how many children they have to support. If your dad is retired you're almost certain to receive what is called the "maximum grant", and so are your brother and sister if they want to go on to college. *Your dad will also be entitled to apply for an additional grant for you from the Miner's Union Welfare Fund. Here, I'll give you a copy of the sixth form prospectus which gives you an outline of what's available, and you can show it to your mum and dad. If they would like to come and discuss it with me, or with Mr Parker (director of sixth form studies), then you can make an appointment for them. All right?'*

A: 'Yes. Thank you, Miss.'

Q: *'Now, what do you need to find out before you can decide whether to take German or music?'*
A: 'Find out if German will be an advantage for the sort of jobs I might be interested in?'

Q :   *'Yes. And?'*
A: 'I'm not sure, Miss.'

Q :   *'Find out if there are any courses or universities which might require a modern language?'*
A: 'Oh. That's right.'

Q :   *'Is there anything else, Michael?'*
A: 'I don't think so, Miss.'

Q :   *'Is there anything you would like to ask me?'*
A: 'Well . . . I was wondering if there was any way I could do one of them in my free time?'

Q :   *'Have you got any free time, Michael?'*
A: 'Well I've got lunchtimes and after school, and I could give up going to the youth club or something.'

Q :   *'I think you'd better find out if it's possible first, and we'd all have to be sure that the rest of your work didn't suffer. Would you be prepared to give something up to do both of them, if it was possible?'*
A: 'Yes, Miss.'

Response:
Q :   *'Right. Then you'd better make a note in your file of the things you're going to check :*
       1 Will a modern language be useful or necessary for jobs in the areas you've mentioned?
       2 Will related courses demand or prefer a modern language?
       3 Can you do either of them in your spare time?
       For number 1, I suggest that you have a look at the chart in the careers library headed 'languages and work'; it's by the side of the biggest

*filing cabinet. For number 2, see Mr Parker; for number 3, Mr Boyce
and Mrs Lees. Then pop back and see me on Wednesday at the same
time as today. Is that nice and clear?'*

A: 'Yes. Thank you, Miss.'

The outcome

When Michael returned he had discovered the following things:

1 Some professional engineering bodies actively encourage the acquisition of a modern language.
2 A modern language is considered 'useful' in all branches of industry and commerce which export goods and services or share contacts, even if only as a basis for 'refresher' courses.
3 Several 'elite' English universities, and some of the Scottish ones, require a modern language as a general entry requirement.
4 Several engineering, and management, degree courses include a year's study abroad, including German industrial and commercial placements.
5 There is no possibility of 'extra' lessons in German because of the tight staffing and the problem of creating a precedent.
6 The head of music is prepared to take an extra group one evening and one lunchtime a week, and in view of Michael's ability and active involvement in music outside of school there is no question that he will cope without any difficulty.

Outcomes

a Michael opted for German, and studied music in his free time.
b The heads of department, head of year, head of careers, the directors of studies and of the sixth form considered this and other cases when reassessing the option blocks for the following year.
c The head of careers considered how the careers programme might be improved to clarify some of the points which had been raised by Michael's case, and others like it.

Analysis of the guidance process

In this case, it would have been easy to tell Michael that he had to opt for German because in the long run it would be better for him. After all, he would still be able to enjoy his music as a leisure activity and even follow it seriously without the O–level. Heavily–pointed advice would almost certainly have achieved the same objective.

A cynical observer would say that in this instance the head of careers was aware of the likely outcome, and simply delayed the inevitable; this is a frequent criticism of 'non–directive' counselling and guidance. The reality of course is that the head of careers has taken Michael through a *decision–making process* by asking him:

– to state the problem as he sees it

- to consider his values in relation to the two subjects and his vocational interests
- to reveal his sources of information and influence
- to reveal any constraints on his choice
- to identify additional information needed
- to consider alternatives
- to find the information for himself
- to decide himself.

Not only has this enabled the head of careers to be fairly certain about Michael's values and motivation, but it has also brought to light a major constraint on his choice and vocational plans – his father's financial concern. Both Michael and his family will be relieved that this doubt has been largely removed – and it has served as a timely reminder that Michael is the first member of his family ever to contemplate further, let alone higher, education. Above all, he has been 'shown the way' but has arrived there under his own steam. In the process, he has discovered a lot for himself and, having made a positive choice and accepted responsibility for it, he is likely to be much more highly motivated towards his German than he would otherwise have been.

Over the next two to four years the aim of the head of careers will be to use the careers education programme and subsequent guidance interviews to make Michael and his fellow students increasingly conscious of problem–solving strategies so that they can become progressively more self–directing, and less dependent upon others for guidance.

Incidentally, this was a fairly typical example of the inter–relatedness of personal, academic and vocational factors. None of them could have been considered in strict isolation from the others, and still satisfactorily resolved the problem.

The Michael West interview is an example of counselling within the guidance process. It was dealing with a specific problem which had arisen and which needed to be resolved before Michael could move forward. In addition to these 'crisis' interviews the guidance programme, in conjunction with the careers education programme, will be checking the stage which each student has reached, and providing appropriate counselling or strategies to help them to move forward. A major tool in this task is the guidance calendar.

A guidance calendar

NB Individual guidance – from a 'chat' to a full interview – will be provided throughout years 3–7 as required. Likely decision points are marked 'D'

Term	Year 3	4	5
AUTUMN	Careers education programme begins Parents informed of content and guidance available	Fourth to fifth year careers provision introduced	Year outlined Work experience 2 Screening interviews Session of three parents' and students' evenings: 1 Moving on 2 Employment/YTS 3 Further education
	Role of careers in 'options' process discussed with head of year, deputies, heads of department	Initial planning for work experience placementsD	Careers interviewsD – 1 Easter leavers 2 summer leavers Initial FE plansD Examinations – parents' evenings, Examination entryD Help with applications
SPRING	Fourth–year. Options programme begins in careers lessons Third year examinations and assessments	Individual plans drawn up for using the conventionD	Summer–leaver careers interviews continue Closing date for some apprenticeshipsD
		CAREERS CONVENTION	
	Parents' evening (Careers staff and officers available to discuss vocational implications of option choices)D Individual interviews	Fourth–year examinations Follow up to careers convention Work experience placements confirmed	Parents' evening for potential sixth form Provisional courses Careers officer briefs Easter leaversD Leavers pack advice
SUMMER	Further interviews as required Options completedD Careers staff discuss personal careers file with students in class, and help with the 'contract'D	Fourth–year parents' evening. Careers staff/officer available JIIG–CAL Work experience Group 1 Careers file checked. Plans for next year reviewedD	Check state of play (Plans, applications, 'back-ups')D CSE examinations Careers officer briefs students Leavers/Returning packs Study leave GCE examinations Sixth–form induction August: results help

A guidance calendar

A two-year cycle   Major decision points are marked [D]

Year 6	One-year student	Common to all	Two–year student
AUTUMN	Induction interviews	Introduction	Careers interviews by request
	Profile style assessments	Introductory parents' evening	
	Careers interviews[D]	Half–term assessments[D]	
		Guidance interviews[D]	
		November resits	
SPRING	**Closing dates** for some apprenticeships[D]	January assessments[D]	CASCAID/JIIG–CAL
		Results of resits[D]	
	Leavers' package	Parents' evening	Oxbridge fourth term?[D]
		O–A/O mocks[D] and *entries*	Higher education forum 1
		Easter assessments[D]	
SUMMER	Letters (report) home	External examinations	Higher education forum 1(continued)
	Careers interviews[D]		Internal examinations
			Careers interviews[D]
			Annual assessments
			Interviews[D]
			Letters home – reports
			End–of–term assessment

Holiday period Decision to return for one or two years	August O–level results[D]	Course changes[D]

Year 7 Two-Year student

AUTUMN HEd forum 2 (past students)	SPRING Mock examinations	SUMMER Letters home – reports
UCCA, polytechnic, C of HE applications[D]	Post-mock review of entry[D]	Examination leave of absence
Careers interviews[D]	Careers interviews[D]	External examinations
15 October Oxbridge *deadline*	15 May UCCA *deadline*[D] for 'firm and provisional' acceptance	Leaving pack
Assessments, pastoral interviews[D]	CAP proceeds	Clearance procedure from college
15 December UCCA *deadline*	Assessments	HOLIDAY PERIOD Circa 15 August – results
Parents evening		FEIS and HEIS, plus school–based service[D]
		Clearing[D]

The guidance calendar is an aid towards identifying the points at which students are likely to require some form of guidance. The number of decision points highlights the major problem facing any guidance teacher. All students are going to be faced with a number of decisions which seem to multiply as they get older. Some students will decide without requiring individual guidance. Others will seek help, even when they can resolve a problem. And there are always some who will need guidance, but will either fail to seek it or not understand how to seek it. The problem is, of course, how to cater for this diversity.

1 Use the careers education programme to prepare students for the various decision points by drawing attention to them. Show them how they can use the information and skills being developed in the lessons to arrive at a decision, and how they can use the guidance system to help them in this process.

2 Use careers lessons – at the appropriate times in the programme – to check plans and to check the basis for decisions which have already been made. This doesn't need to be time–consuming and can easily become a regular feature of 'updating' students' own personal careers records.

3 Give the students their own outline calendar for the year, to keep in their file, showing when deadlines occur and when decisions might have to be made.

4 Use a guidance calendar to remind you of when interventions might be necessary, and when requests for advice might come thick and fast.

None of this needs to take up much of your time. Once the calendar is constructed for each of the years, it is unlikely to need very much – if any – updating for several years.

The 'interventions' and requests for advice require a professional provision of individual interviews and counselling and this is examined in the section which follows.

B Interviewing and counselling

'One-to-one guidance' is a simplistic but useful definition of counselling. It can occur in almost any setting and take the form of a quick 'chat', which might be a simple checking of information, or be in the form of a pre-planned, or 'crisis', interview. Whatever the form or setting, the skills required by the guidance counsellor will be the same.

If we think back to the Michael West case study, the head of careers went through the following process. She *welcomed* Michael, *reassured* him and then *encouraged him to explain* his dilemma. In the process of *listening* to him she sensed that there was another problem complicating the one which he was presenting. By *questioning* him she discovered the various facets of the problem and that Michael needed more information before he could make a decision. She *agreed the appropriate action* with Michael and then *terminated* the interview having *recorded* the details. When Michael returned with the information, *he was able to make a decision*.

Diagram 13 is an expanded version of Carl Rogers' basic counselling model to provide an outline of this process, to define the counsellor's role, and to pinpoint the activities and skills involved.

A counselling situation may begin and end at any one of the five stages shown. In the Michael West case it was necessary to start at the beginning, and to terminate the interview at the end of stage three in order to allow Michael to gather more information. The second interview would have started at stage four, and was able to work through to completion. The head of careers already knew her client and was aware of the outline of the presenting problem in advance. Imagine the task facing a careers officer who has approximately 30 minutes in which to work through a similar process with a virtual stranger. This emphasises the need for the careers officer to become a familiar figure in the period before careers interviews begin and to be armed with as much relevant information as possible for each interview. In the absence of this background, it could take ten minutes or more simply to establish rapport.

The skills needed in the counselling situation are those which involve:
welcoming;
self-awareness;
attending;
observing;
listening;
responding;
questioning;
analysing;
encouraging decision–making;
recording and
monitoring.

Diagram 13   A basic counselling model

Stage		The counsellor's role	Need to be aware of
1 **Establishing rapport**	–	Putting the student at his ease; creating a welcoming setting	Welcome; setting; seating (position and distance); posture; eye to eye contact
2 **Ventilation**	–	Listening to the student and encouraging him to reveal the problem	Minimising distractions/ disturbance; use of encouraging head movements and facial expression; listening; suspension of value–judgement and emotional attachment; managing silence; encouraging responses
3 **Understanding the problem**	–	Checking that the 'presenting problem' is the real problem. Helping the student to fully understand his problem	Use of questions: open, encouraging, non–judgemental. Managing silence; checking problem is understood
4 **Decision– making**	–	Helping the student to make his own decision by helping him through the appropriate stages of decision–making	*Student* to restate problem; consider solutions; advantages/disadvantage implications; decision; action; backup
5 **Terminating the interview**	–	Bringing the interview to a close at the appropriate stage, which might be any one of the five stages	Summarise progress; check action agreed and understood; agree future interview if required; record interview/action/monitor.

(Carl Rogers' model – see *Basic Counselling*, J Shaw, Vernon Scott Associates, 1973)

1 Self–awareness. If you are going to assume a counselling role then you have first to know yourself. As teachers we tend to fall into two categories — 'authoritarian' and 'protective'. Sometimes we gravitate from one to the other with confusing unpredictability. The first category tends towards direction and discipline, the second towards emotional attachment. As individuals, we are bound to have prejudices and preferences. All of these factors will limit our objectivity, and the extent to which we are 'acceptable' in a guidance sense.

The students need a counsellor who is open, honest, accepting and whom they can trust with their ideas and feelings. You have to be aware of your own limitations in this respect and seek to remove them in a counselling situation. If you don't believe that you can set aside your own prejudices and value–judgements when trying to analyse someone else's problem, then you should not consider undertaking guidance work at all. Of course it may be that you are not aware of the extent to which you are directive, over–supportive or prejudiced, and this is where training in interviewing and counselling skills can be invaluable in showing you how to identify your limitations and improve your skills. (Details of relevant training opportunities appear in the section on training.)

2 Welcoming   Really part of the 'attending' process, this skill involves the ability to create a welcoming, non–threatening atmosphere in which the student will feel able to ventilate his problem openly and fully. Anybody who is officially designated as a 'guidance' person is going to be even more busy during their supposedly free time than during that which is set aside for guidance purposes. In a school, breaks and lunchtimes are often the only time when students are free to seek guidance. 'We haven't got long you know', 'Not you again?' and 'Haven't you sorted that out yet?' are understandable responses but unlikely to help the student reveal a serious underlying problem, especially when he may not be aware that it is a problem.

3 Attending   Students are going to need to know that you are actually paying attention to what they are saying, thinking and feeling. Sitting in a position which ensures that you are facing the student, are a 'comfortable' distance from him — not so close as to be overpowering or so far away as to seem remote — and keeping reasonable eye–to–eye contact will all help. Constant interruptions — knocks at the door, telephone calls — have to be eliminated, and even simple distractions like flicking through the file, fiddling with your watch or scribbling notes can suggest that you are not attending. If the position was reversed you would be quick to tell the student to 'pay attention!'

4 Observing   This is the skill of watching a student closely without appearing to do so in order to pick up clues from his general demeanour, facial expressions and body movements, which might reinforce or even contradict what he is saying. A combination of non–verbal clues and verbal inflexions enabled the head of careers to pick up information about Michael's attitude towards the two subjects and to sense that there was also an underlying problem behind the one which he was presenting. Careful observation also helps a counsellor to decide when and how to respond.

5 Listening   This is one of the most important, and among untrained persons the most neglected, of skills. Before you can help the student to understand fully the problem you have to be sure that you understand it yourself. If the head of careers had not listened to everything which Michael said — because after all, she already 'knew' what the problem was – the whole of the problem would not have come to light. As it was, she asked him to explain in his own words, listened and observed without interruption and was consequently in a better position to begin questioning.

In order to listen you have first to forget any pressing worries or tasks of your own. If the first request for this interview gives the remotest impression that it is going to take longer than you can allow — let's assume that you have ten minutes to your next lesson or an appointment with a parent — then it is better to postpone the interview, unless it is a critical one which would justify cancelling your other arrangements or commitments. Having cleared your mind, it is important to concentrate on what is being said and how it is being said. Don't allow your value judgements or sympathy for the student to distract you from following every word and don't be tempted to interrupt or complete statements in order to 'help him along'. Listen to the silences as well; use your powers of observation and any sixth sense which you might have to 'hear' what is not being said, but is almost certainly being expressed.

6 Responding There are two forms of response: those which are intended to confirm that the counsellor is attending and to encourage the student to continue and those which are intended to check what it appears is being said. Head–nodding, smiles and the use of phrases like 'I see', 'Yes' and 'Go on . . .' all fall into the first group of confirming and encouraging responses. Used indiscriminately they will reduce an interview to a shambles, but used selectively and constructively they can help to establish rapport, confidence and fluency of expression on the part of the student.

Responses to content are often questions, but may also be in the form of a restatement of what the interviewer thinks the student has said, means by what they have said, or is feeling. The purpose of such responses is either to check that the impression gained by the counsellor is accurate, or to assure the student that the counsellor understands and empathises (not sympathises) with the point he is making.

When the head of careers responded to Michael's comments about his father's retirement worries by saying: 'I see. And your mum and dad may still have your brother and sister to support at that stage?' she not only proved that she understood and appreciated the problem, but went a stage further by checking out with a rhetorical question whether or not the role of the brother and sister had entered into the discussions between Michael and his parents. As it happened, they had, but it is unlikely that Michael would have revealed that himself without the encouraging response.

7 Questioning If listening is one major part of the process, then questioning is the other. We are used as teachers to the art of asking questions. Unfortunately, they are too often questions to which we know the answers and to which we expect our students to know the answers. In the example above the head of careers used a rhetorical statement of fact, but only as a reinforcement and an exploration of things left unsaid. She made almost every other question as open ended as possible, allowing Michael to speak his mind rather than directing him towards her view of the 'correct response'. Consider the following examples:

– 'Why do you want to do music?'
– 'What do you think, Michael?'
– 'What about German, Michael? Why do you want to take that?'
– 'Have you thought about the kinds of employment you would consider?'
– 'And what about further courses?'

– 'How do you mean, Michael?'

All of these questions require him to consider his own values and to reveal reasons for wanting to choose one solution rather than another. In this sense they are exploratory for both the counsellor and for the student.

The major pitfalls in questioning are:

a Asking leading questions which pressure the student into a particular response, eg 'You don't really want to do them both, do you?' Far better to ask, 'What would you really like to do, if it was possible?'.

b Asking closed questions which have no specific relevance to the problem in hand, and may elicit a single word answer, eg 'Do you like music?' It is already obvious that he does. Far more helpful to ask, 'Why do you like music?' — an 'open' question to which there could be a number of interesting and revealing replies: 'the teacher'; 'it's easy'; 'it helps with my cornet playing'; 'I want to be a musician'; etc.

c Asking too many questions at once. This is a pitfall which also afflicts classroom teachers. Either we change our minds half way through the first question or see the blank look on a score of faces and immediately 'put it another way'. In either case the result is confusion. Try to ask one question at a time and leave time for reflection and response.

d Failing to manage silence. When students are used to teachers answering for them, they may need time to discover that a reply is expected and then more time in which to think about the question and to form an answer. The harder the question is to answer — whether it's because of the complexity of the answer or the depth of honesty needed — the more important the silence in which to put it all together.

Some of the best counsellors I have observed, or been counselled by, were most noticeable by the care with which they chose their questions and their management of silence.

8 Analysing If you are going to be able to take the student through a decision–making process, it follows that you have to be capable of analysing all of the information which you are receiving — verbal and non–verbal — adding it to and checking it against information already received from other sources including the student record, and arriving at an assessment of the situation. Without that skill all of the others are going to be useless, except as a cathartic experience for the student. This skill depends upon how well you have managed all of the other skills, and will improve with experience. Examining case studies, sitting in on other interviews or attending training sessions will certainly help you to develop analytical skills.

9 Encouraging decision–making This is the normal outcome of most vocational guidance interviews. It assumes that the situation has been satisfactorily analysed and checked by the interviewer and is understood by the student, and the student wishes to make a decision. This is the part of the interview which is most likely to approximate the popular view of guidance. The counsellor is 'showing the way' by taking the student through the various stages of decision–making and indicating appropriate sources of information but, as is evident from the Michael West study, the student has the onus of following up the route mapped out by the guide, and of deciding which paths to take. The skill is in 'showing' without 'taking'. The student has to decide an action plan, and take the initiative himself.

10 Recording and monitoring   Recording the important parts of the interview, and action agreed, is a skill of selection in itself. Monitoring the student's progress to see if the action takes place and that the outcome is satisfactory is easily forgotten as the part of the counselling process in which the counsellor has a passive role, but ought to be built into the action agreed by requiring the student to make a brief report back on completion of the task or by a certain date.

NB Interview and counselling skills are so specific, and sometimes confused by accepted teaching styles, that *training ought to be mandatory* for teachers thinking of adding guidance responsibilities to their existing expertise. The *guidelines* offered in this section have been just that. They should not be seen as a sufficient basis for professional vocational guidance.

C Information for careers guidance

i Why and for whom?

Before she began to discuss Michael West's problem with him, the head of careers in our case study read through his school file. There was a lot of information there which helped her to assist Michael, but even so there were facts which emerged during their discussion which were not evident from the file. At the end of the session the head of careers entered a brief résumé of their interview, and included the fact that Michael's father would be retiring during the period that his son might be at university, and was concerned about the financial position; details had been provided for Mr West.

This information is clearly for Michael's benefit and for no one else's. If the head of careers should leave the school, the next person to see Michael in relation to his vocational plans will be aware of the fact that there had been some doubt about him being able to afford to go on to higher education and can ensure that this is no longer a real problem. No information should be kept in a student's personal school file or record card unless it is ultimately for his benefit. This being the case, his parents ought to have access to it if requested, and this would ensure that information could be checked and would be more likely to be based upon evidence rather than upon supposition.

The answer to the questions 'Why?' and 'For whom?' can be summed up as follows:

- **Why? – to enable informed decisions to be made**
- **For whom? – for the student**

Through the following users:	Guidance staff Head/deputies Heads of year/house Careers staff
And to provide information to parents and:	Careers officers; educational welfare and in-care support services; educational psychologists; subject staff; employers; FE and HE admissions tutors etc

ii What information?

The simple answer would be 'Anything which might be helpful in assisting with guidance, and in particular with informed decision–making.' It might be more helpful to list the sort of information which is normally to be found in a school file or on a school record card.
- Full name. Address. Date of birth. Photograph. Date of admission.
- Admission number. Leaving date.
- Name of parents/guardians; occupation; home and emergency phone number.

- Health and medical facts.
- Previous schools.
- Academic record to date including primary school record.
- Reports and assessments; summative profiles (copies).
- Examination results to date.
- Domestic circumstances (where relevant, and with the knowledge of parents).
- Interests, hobbies, leisure activities.
- Membership of clubs, societies.
- Special skills or aptitudes. Awards for achievement of any kind.
- Positions of responsibility — in school or in the community.
- Part–time jobs.
- Work experience.
- Attendance and punctuality. Notes from home.
- Careers interview dates and reports.
- Reports of pastoral/guidance interviews; indication of action agreed.
- Record of applications, interviews, offers. Employment/FE/HE.
- Copies of references and testimonials.
- Note of initial destination and subsequent correspondence.

At first sight there would appear to be a wealth of information here as a basis for guidance. In reality, there are often a number of problems:

1 The information comes from different parts of the system and depends upon a number of compilers. The extent to which the information needed is entered in the file depends upon the relative importance accorded to it by each particular compiler, the amount of time at their disposal and their perception of record systems generally.

2 Fears and confusion about confidentiality can result in gaps in information, and cryptic messages: "Serious DP. AcWork suffers. see JP". Apparently, there has been a serious domestic problem which has affected academic work, and JP — who, incidentally, left last year — knows all of the details. But at least there is a record and the student concerned should be able to fill in the details better than anyone.

3 The file or record card is usually held centrally by the head of year or head of house. Your room or office may be some distance away, filing cabinets may be locked in the absence of their keeper, and there is occasionally a tendency for keepers to regard such information as their own private property or sacred trust, to be made available to others only under extreme duress.

In the real world, rather than in an ideal situation, information may therefore be:

- incomplete
- incomprehensible
- inaccessible.

The solution is to work to improve the situation and to ensure in the meantime that you have the information which you, the careers officer and other users, will need for vocational guidance purposes.

ii(a) **Philosophy**   You have to play your part in reinforcing or developing the philosophy within the school that the personal, academic and vocational aspects of a student's life are interdependent and virtually inseparable, and that information regarding any of these areas must be available to all guidance staff.

It may be necessary for you to demonstrate the importance of personal and academic information to you and other vocational guidance staff by using actual case studies from within the school. Always make it a habit to explain the reasons for requests for information — to subject or tutorial staff — yourself, rather than through a third party, both as a courtesy and as a reinforcement of the system.

It will also help if you can demonstrate how information gathered by careers staff can be of assistance to other staff. It is frequently the case that in the final years at school the careers staff have the most complete picture of individual students, and heads of year/house may come to depend heavily upon the information provided by careers staff for their guidance, references, and testimonials.

ii(b) **The System:** collection, collation, storage, retrieval.

In terms of much of the information listed in my example of a school record, you are unlikely to have much responsibility for the way in which the information is gathered, sorted, filed and accessed, but you can suggest improvements in the name of accuracy and efficiency. From the point of view of the providers of information there is almost always too much paper involved and far too much duplication. Get together with the heads of year and use your guidance calendar and their pastoral calendar to determine what information each of you will need, and when. Try to combine the paperwork/forms wherever you can, so that subject staff or tutors only have to provide the same information once. Agree the timing and who will distribute and collect the information, how it will be recorded and determine that it will be available for joint use.

A case study

During the fifth year at high school the following people will need information about each of the fifth year students:

1 the head of year – for guidance and testimonials
2 the head of careers – for guidance and references
3 the careers officer – for guidance and placement
4 the head of sixth form – for guidance and course planning.

If each of these users produced a form to be completed for their own use then the subject staff — and more particularly the form tutors — would be understandably unenthusiastic by the time the fourth request reached them. Nor would it improve their humour to discover that virtually the same information was required by all four users.

Diagram 14 (overleaf) presents a picture of the information which is normally required at this stage, the likely compilers and some of their sources. If you think that this is something of an exaggeration, I can assure you that it is not. Every year we have to complete scores of references on pro-formas which are far more detailed in their questioning.

The case for devising a single form — or guidance profile — to be completed in stages, is inescapable.

During the students' final term, subject staff would complete their sections and give estimated grades; the fourth year form tutors could then complete their sections and pass them on to the careers staff for them to add their own observations and vocational input. The head of year would check them against the school record file and add relevant information. Before the fifth year careers interviews began, staff could be asked if they wished to alter their estimates and students could provide any information themselves about holiday work, changed circumstances or changing aspirations. As soon as internal mock exam results became available, estimates could be revised. A copy of the form/summative profile would be made available to the careers officer, and the original would remain in the school record file for guidance, testimonials and references.

Diagram 14	**Information for fifth year**	*Likely compiler*
Circumstances	domestic and others, affecting inclination/opportunity	Form tutor, head of year
Health	medical history, disabilities, vision, hearing, allergy	Form tutor, school nurse, head of year, careers staff
Physical characteristics	physique, speech, appearance	Form tutor
Physical aptitude	Dexterity, co-ordination, reactions, strength, senses	Nurse, careers staff, subject staff, + DAT (aptitude tests)
Mental aptitude	all verbal and non-verbal aptitudes, language, spatial, numerical, mechanical, clerical, memory, perceptional	Head of year, subject staff, careers staff, (DATs)
Academic achievement and potential	examination and assessment results to date, estimated grades for exams pending, potential for further study and/or training	Subject staff (Examinations, assessments, profiles)
Personality	energy, impulsiveness, thoroughness, sociability, sensitivity, honesty, co-operativeness, dominance, independence, resilience, self–control, ambition	Form tutor, subject staff, careers staff, head of year, (psychometric tests)
Sources and degree of motivation	value attached to material success, practical objectives, security, caring, gaining attention or influence, discovery, the arts, the environment	Careers staff, form tutors, (profiles/psychometric tests)

Interests and hobbies	interests and activities, achievements, positions of responsibility in and out of school	Form tutor, careers staff, head of year
Experience of employment or voluntary work	evidence of part-time jobs, work experience, voluntary activities	Form tutor, careers staff, head of year
Vocational aspirations	short term and long term vocational plans, tentative or realistic? Employment/FE/YTS. Job families	Careers staff

But there is another way. We have already established that all of this information is for the sole purpose of helping the student to make decisions wisely. Surely the aim of education is to enable a student to become independent and self–directing in relation to his life — its opportunities and responsibilities — when compulsory schooling ends? Well, it happens that the student is not only the focus, but also the major source of all of the information we seek to compile.

Students provide us with information (some of which we check for accuracy) which is then assessed — sometimes objectively and sometimes subjectively — before we store it away for later use. It may be as much as three years before the student is reminded that the information exists; he may never be reminded. The same is true of information which we give the student about himself.

If we really hope to encourage self–awareness among our students, that information ought to be part of their own personal file; part of a consciously dynamic process of growth. Certainly we need a record of it for guidance purposes, but the information should also stay in their possession. That is what the *personal careers file* mentioned in the careers education programme is all about.

Encouraging — even requiring — students to keep a record of their personal, academic and vocational development and of any information relevant to their vocational decisions, has the following advantages:

1 Students begin to see the relevance of their school work, and of their personal and social development, to their future life and life choices.

2 As a result they are more likely to become self–motivated in their learning activities.

3 Because they are shown what information they need and how it may be used, they are likely to become self–directing far sooner than if we act as the sole custodians and interpreters of that information.

4 Because they are better informed they are likely to be more realistic in their aspirations far sooner. (This does not mean that ambition is suppressed — quite the reverse!)

5 All of the information which they need in order to make applications for employment, training and further or higher education is instantly

available to them. (Sometimes the information required on an application form can be even more comprehensive than that asked of the referee. The BBC, for example, has asked for medical history, including specific notification of any history of 20 named diseases and conditions.)

6 If students are regularly compiling information about themselves, it will be that much easier for form tutors, careers staff and other users to elicit that information for guidance purposes.

In the CRAC unit *My Job Application File* there is a sample personal record called *My Personal File*, which covers personal history, educational history, school activities, spare–time activities, references, work experience and medical history. The reasons for the information required in each section is explained and copies of eight actual job application forms are given to highlight the vocational need for such information.

Used in conjunction with a programme of careers education designed to develop self–awareness, awareness of opportunities and the life skills we have considered, this personal record becomes not only an exercise in information gathering but also a tool for guidance and, more importantly, for self-guidance.

In schools where continuous assessment or profiling is part of the system, this personal file would be supplemented by information from end–of–term or end–of–year summative statements agreed by staff and students.

This has to be a far better, more open, honest and motivating method of recording than that which depends upon secrecy rather than confidentiality. There is no justification, for example, for the common practice of refusing to give students in their final year some indication of the grades which they are believed to be capable of and the grades which they are currently expected to achieve. We expect them to make applications for jobs, training schemes, further and higher education, many of which depend not only on passes but upon specific grades, and yet there are still teachers who refuse even to give their students an indication of the range within which they are likely to come. This reflects a lack of confidence on the part of teachers in their own professional judgement, and it acts as a serious handicap and de–motivator for many students. The examination system may be unreliable, but our students are entitled to a professional statement of their relative achievement and potential, as we see it, and based upon evidence. As teachers we pass judgements all the time, and when it comes to the crucial point of making a prediction based upon those judgements we wave a white flag and plead caution, leaving the students in no–man's–land.

Low estimates are only discouraging when they come as a surprise, and if they come as a surprise to the teacher then the teacher has failed to monitor and assess progress. If regular and honest assessments have reflected a student's ability they will almost always accept the estimate which follows. If they don't, experience shows that the determination to prove the teacher wrong becomes the most powerful motivator that student has had for some time.

Wherever the record requires a predictive or judgemental assessment the key words are 'evidence' and 'honesty'. Nobody can be expected to do better than that, and students are well aware of that fact. What they cannot accept — and rightly so — are assessments based upon feelings as opposed to evidence, and judgements about them which are kept secret.

If this point appears to have been laboured it is because one of your battles may be to persuade staff of the importance of being open and honest with students in relation to assessments and records of any kind, but if students are to become self–directing we have a duty to give them all of the information which they need and to show them how to use it to advantage.

Storage and retrieval   The most popular systems consist of wallet–style files, incorporating record cards, which are kept in the office of the head of house or head of year. Because of the importance and confidentiality of these files the cabinets are usually kept locked in the absence of the 'keeper', spare keys being held by the bursar, or head and deputies.

Where access is limited by time, distance, or other problems, the careers staff often maintain their own card index system which contains the most important details only, for each student, as a 'memory jogger' for planning and administrative purposes. (For counselling purposes the school file or personal record card should always be available.) A simple example of such a card appears below. Details of vocational interviews appear on the reverse side.

Surname: Welsh   **Christian names:** Jane, Mary

Form: 5.3

Date of birth: 4/2/68

Easter/Summer leaver

Subjects/level and actual grades/estimates if known

English language	'O' – C June '83	Chemistry	C
English literature	'O' – C/D	Biology 'O'	B
Mathematics	'O'/CSE – D/1	Home economics	C
French	CSE – 2	Art	B
History	'O' – B		

Hobbies/interests/achievements:

Health: Good; mild hay fever; appendicitis first year

Work experience: Three weeks – Masons (clerical) July '83. Paper round.

Vocational plans/applications:
Nursing (SRN) grade 11.
Applying – A-levels or pre-nursing.
Careers interview 8/11/83

Filed alphabetically or alphabetically by form, in a box or filing cabinet in the careers office, these cards can be great timesavers, but should never be allowed to replace the use of the main file or the student's own personal file.

Computers are beginning to be used for record storage and retrieval in colleges and it is only a matter of time before they become the main system of central records in schools. This would mean that careers staff would have to have a terminal screen and keyboard in their office for guidance interviews; the computer could also be used, of course, for the computer programmes mentioned in the careers education section.

The current fear about computer records is that of security. There is no reason for supposing that school records held in this way would be any more or less secure than those currently held in filing cabinets and cardboard wallets, unless of course the system is keyed in to a mainframe system through the telephone network. In this case, it would be possible for a computer 'expert' who had gained access to the codes used to call up student records through a modem or coupling device, and copy or tamper with the contents. The fantasy of *War Games* is not a fantasy at all. There has been a case of twelve-year-olds accessing mark lists from a college records system, using codes swopped around at a computer club.

The system does not need to be this vulnerable. There are straightforward methods of excluding and protecting confidential information stored in this way; the problem is that either the 'locks' are never fitted or the 'keys' – in the form of codes – are left where they can be picked up.

Providing that advice is sought and precautions are taken, there is no reason why this fast and instantly available system should not be used.

CRAC has produced a *Careers Record System* designed to provide a comprehensive picture of a student's progress and developing vocational interests. This could form a useful starting point for developing your own system – computerised or otherwise.

Profiles

No consideration of information–gathering and recording would be complete without mention of profiling. A profile is basically a record of student achievement which may or may not lead towards a certificate or alternative statement of achievement. There are two forms of profile:

1 A *formative* profile is one which is built up progressively over time, with the active participation of the student, and which is intended to reinforce and monitor progress through an agreed curriculum;
2 A *summative* profile is one which provides a record or statement of attainment at a given point in time; it may or may not form the basis of a certificate.

There is a lot of debate at the moment about the relative value of summative profiles based on continuous assessment compared with straightforward examination results, as an indicator of attainment. There is also concern about the amount of time which profiling can take up as part of a formative process. Detailed examination of the issues, and examples of practice in the use of profiles, is given in the Further Education Curriculum Review and Development Unit (FEU) publication entitled *Profiles*, and available free from the DES. Although this document deals essentially with profiles for training and education in further education, the same principles apply. Swindon and City of Sheffield education departments have published details of experience of profiling in schools, and the Schools Council published an independent evaluation of the Swindon scheme in 1979. The DES has also set out guidelines for summative profiles for all school leavers in the document *Records of Achievement* (1984).

The following points are very important in relation to profiles:
- objectives must be very clearly defined
- students, as well as staff, have to be able to understand the objectives
- those objectives which are specific to a subject area or profiling period should take preference over those which are common to all areas and profiling periods
- if the profile is to be truly formative in the student's development and learning process it should be continuous – rather than hurriedly compiled as the deadline approaches – and be a matter of negotiation between teacher and student, with areas of disagreement over assessment noted
- evidence must be provided to substantiate statements
- each profiling period should be long enough to allow development to take place
- the organisation of time in the school day and in the teacher's working pattern needs to be re-allocated to accommodate profiling
- a substantial programme of in-service education and training is needed to enable staff to use profiling to the maximum advantage for the student and for themselves
- the *advantages* of profiling are that the students become more highly motivated, self-motivated and conscious of what the learning process is about; the relationship between staff and student becomes more open, honest, human and productive.

NB   The personal record suggested earlier in this section is in reality a personal profile, built up with guidance from the careers staff. It is formative in terms of self-awareness, opportunity awareness, and all of the related skills; summative in its use for decision-making (in particular for making applications) and in its potential use in compiling a record of achievement.

Computer–assisted guidance

In the section on resources, mention was made of psychometric tests, interest guides, computer systems like CASCAID and JIG-CAL, and computer kits like COMJOB which include the elements of information, interest guide and test of occupational knowledge. The advantages which computers offer in terms of speed, ease of use when instructions and checks are built into a program, ease of response correction and availability of printout for personal analysis and follow–up, make it an attractive tool for guidance purposes. The ease with which children of all ages and levels of ability adapt to the use of appropriate programs on computer, and the pupil–centred nature of computer response to student response and vice versa, also make it an enjoyable learning method.

In subject-based curriculum areas the major problems which are inhibiting innovation are:

1 the cost of hardware
2 Lack of suitable software—too much is low level drill and practice
3 Shortage of in–service training for staff

In careers education and guidance 1 and 3 (above) are relevant but by no means as serious. For guidance and information purposes a single computer located in the careers room, office or library would suffice in the first instance. The programs available at the moment are not dependent on computing experience for their use and are exploratory and truly 'interactive', rather than simply reinforcing factual learning. The CCDU/COIC computing project offers short courses for staff and the expertise needed for operation rather than programming skills can be acquired very quickly.

The important points to remember in using computer programs for *guidance* purposes are as follows:

1 You must distinguish between those which are intended to give or to test factual information; those which are designed to discover innate traits; and those which are designed to relate a student's self-concept, at a given moment, to his occupational concept or to occupational opportunities.
2 You must be fully aware of the limitations of interest guides and questionnaires—as well as their advantages—and that the time involved in using them effectively is far greater than that required for their completion. Follow–up by a member of staff to ensure that the implications are understood and assimilated by the student is likely to exceed time taken to work through the program.
3 You must identify the relevant steps which each student should take after completing a program, check that they have been taken and relate them to the original responses made by the student.

All of this means that you have to have an intimate knowledge of the various programs; should have been trained in the use of sophisticated systems like JIIG-CAL; expect to spend more rather than less time on guidance; and be aware that whilst the operation of the programs by the student is an individual and self–directing one, that of interpretation requires your special guidance skills in conjunction with his.

Until computers become more readily available you will have to be very selective about the programs you purchase and develop; beware of their use becoming unconsciously restricted to a small number of keen students, rather than those most in need of the programs available, and continue to use OCL, JIIG-CAL, *Computajob* systems in 'batch mode' to ensure blanket coverage.

A detailed account of different systems has not been given because the only way really to find out about them is to see them in action and then undertake a training course where appropriate—JKIs, CASCAID (for careers officers), JIIG-CAL. The advantages of CASCAID and JIIG-CAL are that they both take students through a process of self–assessment, a statement of values and an analysis of the relationship between their own self–concept and their apparent suitability or unsuitability for certain occupations. In the process, they have usually gained greater self–awareness, awareness of the range and nature of opportunities with which they may be compatible and exercised some information and communication skills. What is also evident is that where this exercise is not part of a continuous programme of careers education and guidance, the point of the analysis can quickly become forgotten, the underlying skills are less likely to have become consciously assimilated and the process in fact turns out to have been a narrow job–elimination exercise, useful in itself as a prelude to the careers interview, but neither cost–effective in terms of time, nor the valuable learning experience which it ought to be.

iv   Careers guidance for the physically, mentally and educationally handicapped

The Education Act of 1981 defined children with special educational needs as those who experience exceptional difficulty in learning relative to children of the same age, and those children with physical disabilities which hinder their learning in a normal school setting.

The act makes it the duty of local education authorities—subject to certain conditions—to see that such children are educated wherever possible in an ordinary school.

It will be some time before a general integration of children with and without registered disabilities takes place. In some authorities, however, experiments in integration were taking place before the act and many pilot projects are already under way. The evidence of improved confidence and accelerated learning alone has borne out the findings of the Warnock Report, and it has been estimated that 75% of children currently registered in need of special provision will be integrated into normal schools. The important implications for careers staff appear to be as follows:

a **Identification**   Even in the normal school at present there is ample evidence from careers officers of children suffering from disabilities which positively restrict their vocational choices, but who have not been identified as such by the school. There are several problems here. A shift towards selective medical screening means that some minor disabilities are never identified until young people report for pre–employment medicals. In some schools the information exists but has not been passed on to careers staff or the careers officer. This may be because the system is inefficient or fragmented, because the member of staff responsible does not consider the disability to be severe enough to be worth mentioning, or because the member of staff is over–protective towards children with disabilities.

If this is the case before the act is implemented, there is a real danger that minor disabilities will be disregarded altogether in the face of more obvious handicaps. Some of the minor disabilities which do have vocational implications are mild asthma, colour blindness and other eye problems, partial deafness, diabetes, petit mal epilepsy, dyslexia and arthritis.

Clearly, medicals ought to be more frequent and comprehensive. School records must include educational, medical and other disabilities and be readily available to careers guidance staff. Information must be passed on from primary to secondary school and from secondary to further education.

b **Information** Guidance staff have to have up-to-date information about the vocational implications of any disability, however slight it may seem to be. The specialist careers officer who deals with young disabled persons will be delighted to give you up-to-date hard information about opportunities, rather than have to crisis counsel a disappointed school leaver whose long–held ambition has been dashed following the medical. Equally, inaccurate pessimistic misinformation can unfairly lower students' expectations and limit their opportunities. As Warnock becomes implemented in your school you will have the duty to find out what the realistic alternatives are for individual disabled students, concentrate on their abilities and raise their expectations to the limits of the possible. To do that you are going to have to work closely with the relevant careers officer and support agencies, and help to create wider opportunities in the community for these students.

c **Education and guidance** Integration aims at raising the self–esteem, confidence and levels of learning competence of children with special educational needs, and raising the awareness of other children with regard to the abilities and needs of those of their peers who have disabilities. Careers education—particularly when it includes social and life skills—offers a marvellous vehicle for achieving these ends. Sensitively handled, the exploration of self–awareness, coping skills, communication skills, personal relationships etc, with a mixed group of children with and without special needs, could greatly accelerate the process of integration. Badly handled, it could set back the development of confidence and self–esteem in the disabled. This is one area of the curriculum where research and training are urgently needed.

Guidance for children with disabilities tends to be much more explicitly a combination of educational and personal guidance. It is essential that the process of vocational guidance should start earlier for them than for other pupils. In special schools the option choices facing pupils tends to be much narrower than that in normal schools. In the normal school, options for fourth–year courses have considerable vocational implications for pupils with disabilities. This is one area in which TVEI could present an excellent opportunity for many such children—but not for all of them. Individual vocational guidance will have to start in the third year, and ought to include an interview or case conference with the specialist careers officer and parents present. At all of the important decision-making stages this ideal situation ought to become the norm. This is one area where special provision will still have to be made in terms of time and personnel.

d **Employment and training**   The current position for children with special educational needs who have reached the statutory school leaving age, appears to be as follows:

- Standards of educational achievement are rising.
- The number staying on in 'special' sixth forms, or transferring to integrated sixth forms, is rising.
- The number of further education and training courses suitable for these students is rising.
- The rise in youth unemployment appears to have reduced the opportunities for young people with disabilities far more than for young people without. This is partly because operative and craft level jobs have been hit hardest by the recession and by new technology, and partly because of entry qualification 'inflation'.
- The proportion of YTS placements in industry and commerce seems to be lower than that which obtained under the YOP scheme. A larger proportion of these young people are being offered community projects, local authority YTS placements or further education as their alternatives.
- The unemployment 'bulge' for young people with disabilities is tending to emerge a little later than for others, at age 19.
- The government–funded Out Work Unit Project which is exploring ways in which computer–based technology can offer opportunities for paid employment for some people with disabilities could, if extended to young persons, offer more scope.

While it is to be hoped that some of these trends may be reversed quite quickly, it is important for aspiring careers teachers to know that they exist and to remain fully informed of current trends for all of their students, with or without special educational needs.

PART 5

Training

i The need for training

It should be clear by now that careers education and guidance is a crucial part of the process of education. There is certainly nothing mystical about it, but the assumption that training for this particular field is unnecessary is surely untenable. Throwing a man into still water may be an interesting and efficient way of teaching him to swim, but he may drown, and when the waters become a raging torrent ...

Anyone who doubts the metaphor should spend some time with a careers teacher and see for themselves the range of skills which are required, the unpredictability of demands made by the students and outside agencies, and the flood of information—much of it heralding yet more changes in entry levels, recruitment practices, dates of application, training schemes, eligibility etc.

There has to be a secure foundation of aims, objectives, principles and guidance and management skills just to cope with the task. Given that—and experience—there is a chance of consolidating and developing expertise. Anyone who thinks that they no longer need any training is probably stagnating.

ii Types of training available

The field of careers and guidance training is as much a shifting one as the current employment scene, but the following types of courses are typical of those available at the moment:

ii(a) Courses leading to certificates or diplomas

These are some of the courses which can be considered to be a thorough and organised introduction at present. Approaches and philosophies may differ slightly, but the essential requirements—the provision of awareness and skills—are there in all of them.

Edge Hill College of Higher Education
Ormskirk
Lancashire L39 4QP
Telephone 0695 75171

Diploma in advanced studies in education (Counselling and careers work)	1 year (full-time)
Interviewing and assessing in careers education	1 year (part-time)
College certificate of advanced studies in careers education in the 1980s	1 year (part-time)
Pre-vocational education	Six weeks (full-time)

Hatfield Polytechnic
PO Box 109
College Lane
Hatfield
Hertfordshire AL10 9AB
Telephone 07072 68100 ex 346

Diploma in careers education and guidance   2 years (part-time)

University of Manchester
Department of Education
Manchester M13 9PL
Telephone 061–273 7121

Diploma in guidance and counselling in education   1 year (part-time)

West London Institute of Higher Education
Gordon House
300 St. Margaret's Road
Twickenham
Middlesex TW1 1PT
Telephone 01–891 0121

Diploma in guidance and counselling   1 year (full-time)
     2 years (part-time)

King Alfred's College
Sparkford Road
Winchester
Hampshire SO22 4NR
Telephone 0962 62281

Certificate in careers education   1 term
Certificate in guidance and counselling   1 term

Worcester College of Higher Education
Henwick Grove
Worcester WR2 6AJ
Telephone 0905 428080

Careers education and guidance   1 term

College of Ripon and York St John
Lord Mayor's Walk
York YO3 7EX
Telephone 0904 56771

Guidance and counselling   1 term

ii(b) National courses of short duration

Not everyone is fortunate enough to be able to gain secondment for the
year, term or even for part–time courses requiring one day or half a day a
week. Falling rolls has had the effect of producing more teachers willing
to retrain for guidance and counselling skills, but redeployment is not an
ideal motivation for this work and cash limits seem to be falling as fast as

the rolls. Short courses certainly help to fill this gap in provision, and can prove to be stimulating refreshers and updaters for experienced careers staff.

There are a number of providers in the field, but the following can certainly be recommended:

CRAC courses

As part of its service in the development of guidance work, CRAC runs an annual programme of national courses in careers education and guidance. Usually situated in major cities on the main motorway and train links, they offer one day—and several two to three day—courses covering anything from *An introduction to careers education* to *Guidance and the disadvantaged student.*

In conjunction with NICEC—which is jointly sponsored by CRAC and the Hatfield Polytechnic—CRAC also offers a number of training modules to LEAs and other training agencies. The modules are provided in the LEAs' own accommodation—often teachers' centres—and are tutored by NICEC's academic or field staff. One of the great advantages of these modules is that it brings together all of the practitioners—experienced and novice—within an authority or institution so that a common philosophy begins to emerge, and firm contacts can be made for self–help. Another advantage is that the modules can be modified or purpose–built to suit special needs. If you have the beginnings of a careers teachers' workshop or group but have no in–service provision, you could begin by persuading the authority to consider booking one of these modules as a springboard for your own development.

NACGT Courses

The National Association of Careers and Guidance Teachers has in recent years offered seminars and arranged summer schools for careers teachers, where the emphasis has been on participative activity to develop existing skills.

ICO courses

The Institute of Careers Officers has its own strong training programme, and arranges seminars and courses annually which are open to careers teachers.

Life skills and study skills courses

Courses are now available from private and educational consultancies covering both of these areas, and usually lasting one or two days.

ii(c) Local consortia

In some areas of the county, careers teachers, careers officers and local authority advisers have formed together to co-ordinate in–service training for careers education and guidance. This has included the provision of central courses and the training of experienced practitioners as potential trainers on local and area courses. The first—and most fully developed—is the Yorkshire and Humberside consortium, and the North West Careers Consortium has been in existence for over five years.

Courses tend to be similar in duration and content to short courses already mentioned, and are tailored to meet local needs.

ii(d) **National projects**

At any one time there are likely to be several major projects concerned with improving training and practice in careers education and guidance. At the time of writing two notable ones are:

TRACE – the Schools' Council *Training for and approaches to careers education* project

The aim of the project is to use groups of teachers in five LEAs selected for their diversity in order to define. and evaluate different approaches to careers education and the provision of training for careers teachers. A handbook reporting the major outcomes of the project will be preceded by dissemination of helpful information and strategies as they become available.

The CCDU/COIC training project

The Counselling and Career Development Unit at Leeds University and the Careers and Occupational Information Centre have joined together in a three–year project to provide short in–service training courses. The two day course—*The uses of computers in careers education*—is one of the first to become available.

ii(e) **Consultancy services**

The National Institute for Careers Education and Counselling (NICEC), in addition to providing modular short courses, also provides a consultancy service to improve the effectiveness of existing systems in schools and colleges, and to provide research or training for specific institutions.

ii(f) **Self–help**

Local careers workshops—usually made up of careers teachers and careers officers—often provide a valuable self–help service which may only be at the level of a 'talking–shop' but may also reach the dizzy heights of building up their own resource centre and training schemes. Below are listed the aims and objectives of one such group which is typical of many groups throughout this region.

Leigh Area Careers Teachers and Careers Officers Support Group

Membership		Open to any staff of schools or careers service in Leigh, Atherton and Tyldesley.
Aims	i	Mutual support in the sharing of information, materials, training, experience, liaison, contacts and sources, in order to further effective careers education and guidance in member institutions.
	ii	Liaison with other groups within the borough to the same ends.

Objectives

i   To review programmes in member schools as a source of information, and with a view to adopting or adapting ideas used by colleagues.

ii   To compare facilities:
- timetable time
- non–teaching time
- staffing
- equipment
- other resources
- careers across the curriculum links

to help in formulating individual policies and to provide hard information to add weight to suggested improvements.

iii   To arrange for the sharing of materials and information through a careers resource centre in the teachers' centre, and to arrange joint projects eg a video—*Your Careers Service.*

iv   To review teachers' work with careers officers in order to facilitate joint endeavours.

v   To arrange visits of common interest.

vi   To propose and support in–service training within the borough.

Meetings   Not less than twice per term; venue to be in member schools on a rotating basis.

Postscript

Careers education and guidance as defined in this book seeks to accomplish an important task—that of preparing young people to enter an adult world with the awareness and skills which they need to be self–directing and self–motivating. That task cannot be accomplished in isolation from the rest of their formative experience. Tacking 'careers' on to the end of the curriculum of compulsory education is an inadequate solution to the problem of transition into a complex and changing environment. Unless the whole of the curriculum, and its associated learning strategies, are geared towards preparing children to become self–directing and caring adults, then any interventions by single departments will be disappointing in terms of lasting impact.

'God, grant me the serenity to accept the things I cannot change,
The courage to change the things I can,
And the wisdom to know the difference.'

Appendix I Book lists

The context

Educational and Economic Activity of Young People Aged 16–19 years, in England and Wales from 1973–74 to 1981–82	– DES Statistical Bulletin 2/83
Review of the Economy and Employment	– Warwick University Institute of Employment Research (1983)
Technology, Choice and the Future of Work	– British Association for the Advancement of Science (1978)
Future Shock	– Alvin Toffler (1971) Pan
The Collapse of Work	– Clive Jenkins and Barrie Sherman (1979) Eyre Methuen
Leisure Shock	– Clive Jenkins and Barrie Sherman (1981) Eyre Methuen
Recruitment in the '80s	– Personnel Management (April 1978)
Career Development in Britain	– A G Watts; Donald E Super, Jennifer M Kidd (1981) CRAC
New Training Initiative	– MSC (1981)
A View of the Curriculum	– DES (1980) HMSO
The School Curriculum	– DES and Welsh Office (1981)
A Basis for Choice	– FEU (June 1979)
Changing Schools – Changing Curriculum	– ed M Galton, B Moon (1983) Harper and Row
Freedom to Learn for the Eighties	– Carl Rogers (1983) Charles Merrill

Roles and Systems

Practical Approaches to Careers Education	– Catherine Avent (1974, 3rd edition 1978) CRAC/Hobsons
A Practical Handbook of Careers Education and Guidance	– ed R Heppell (1973) Careers Consultants
The Implications of School Leaver Unemployment for Careers Education in Schools	– A G Watts NICEC Occasional Paper 1 (1979) CRAC
Career Development in Britain	– ed A G Watts, Donald E Super, Jennifer M Kidd (1981) CRAC
Guided Career Exploration	– D E Super, J A Bowlsbey (1979) Psychological Corporation, New York

Schools, Careers and Community	– Bill Law and AG Watts (1977) Church Information Office

Methods

Exercises in Personal and Careers Development	– Barrie Hopson and Patricia Hough (1973) CRAC/Hobsons Press
Exercises (and Further Exercises) in Careers Education	– D R Cleaton (1976, 1977) Careers Consultants
Life Skills Teaching	– Barrie Hopson and Mike Scally (1981) McGraw Hill
Schools Council Careers Education and Guidance Handbooks	– G Reece and J Storey (1983) Longman Group
Active Tutorial Work, Books 1-6	– Health Education Council (1979-83) Basil Blackwell
Choosing Logically, Using Effectively (CLUE)	– COIC (1980)
Life Skills Teaching Programmes no 1	– Barrie Hopson and Mike Scally (1980) Life Skills Associates
Life Skills Teaching Programmes no 2	– Barrie Hopson and Mike Scally (1982) Life Skills Associates

Resources

Choosing Logically, Using Effectively	– COIC (1980)
EEC Transition from School to Working Life Project	– City of Sheffield Education Department (1979-1982)
Practical Approaches to Careers Education	– Catherine Avent (1974, 3rd edition 1978) CRAC/Hobsons Press
Work Experience in the School Curriculum	– S Holmes, I Jamieson, J Perry (1984) SCIP/Trident Trust

Guidance

Practical Guidance in Schools	– Rita Howden and Harry Dowson (1973) Careers Consultants
Careers Guidance; Practice and Problems	– ed Ray Jackson (1973) Arnold
The British Journal of Guidance and Counselling	– CRAC/Hobsons
Basic Counselling	– J Shaw (1973) Vernon Scott Associates

On Becoming a Person	– Carl Rogers (1961) Houghton Mifflin
Tutoring	– John Miller (1982) NICEC/FEU
Profiles	– FEU (1982)
Practical Aspects of Guidance	– D R Cleaton and R J Foster (1982) Careers Consultants

Training

NICEC Training and Development Bulletin	– NICEC (available by subscription)

Appendix 2

JOB SEARCH computer program

The program, designed for Commodore VIC 20 BASIC, takes a student through the stages represented in the diagram and, at each relevant stage, pinpoints the location of the appropriate information in the careers library by means of a flashing symbol on an outline map of the library.

If they wish, students can call up the index and use the program simply to locate information rather than to go through the search procedure.

For the sake of this example only a limited amount of information has been included, but the program is capable of expansion to cover as much information as your library might hold.

It took a 12-year-old with less than 18 months' computer experience under one-and-a-half hours to complete – unaided. There are many similar guidance and information programmes, interest guides and decision–making games and simulations which you could construct and a lot of computer studies students looking for ideas for constructive programs to submit as part of their O–level and A–level courses. Why not use the abilities of your students to help produce programs from which they and their peers will benefit?

NB Bear in mind you will be fortunate to have more than one computer at the disposal of your department, so it makes sense to concentrate, at first, on programs which will benefit the majority of students, in a single user mode. These will tend to be guidance and information programs, rather than games programs.

```
0 REMTHIS PROGRAM IS A     GARETH ROGERS        PRODUCTION
1 A$="JOB SEARCH      - 1":BA=0
2 PRINT"○":FORV=1TO10:PRINTA$:FORC=1TO100:NEXTC,V
6 GOTO10
10 PRINT"○":PRINTA$
11 PRINT"■○■      INDEX"
12 PRINT"■■■A.FLOW CHART■":PRINT
13 PRINT"■B.MAP■":PRINT
14 PRINT"■C.STAGE OF FLOWCHART■":PRINT"■■WHICH DO YOU WANT ?"
15 GETANS$:IFANS$=""THEN15
16 IFANS$="A"THEN102
17 IFANS$="B"THEN250
18 IFANS$="C"THEN20
19 GOTO10
20 PRINT"○":PRINTA$
21 PRINT"■A.BOX FILE "
22 PRINT"B.NO FURTHER ED.      "
23 PRINT"C.FURTHER ED.      "
25 GETANS$:IFANS$=""THEN25
26 IFANS$="A"THEN110
27 IFANS$="B"THEN222
28 IFANS$="C"THEN122
30 IFANS$=" "THEN10
100 GETN$:IFN$=" "THENRETURN
101 GOTO100
102 PRINT"○"
103 PRINT"GOTO COIC CLASS LISTS":PRINT
104 PRINT"           OR":PRINT
105 PRINT"        SIGNPOSTS.":PRINT
106 PRINT" IDENTIFY REF. CODE"
107 PRINT"  FOR CHOSEN CAREER"
108 PRINT""
110 PRINT"          \/"
111 PRINT"■        BOX FILE "
112 PRINT"         /  \"
113 PRINT"        /    \"
114 PRINT"     NO.        YES"
115 PRINT"FURTHER ED FURTHER ED"
116 PRINT"■■■ HIT Y OR N PLEASE"
117 GETYN$:IFYN$=""THEN117
118 IFYN$=" "THEN10
119 IFYN$="Y"THEN122
120 IFYN$="N"THEN222
121 GOTO102
122 PRINT"○"
123 PRINT"SEE F.E/H.ED HANDBOOKS"
124 PRINT"■■ RANGE LENGTH NATURE"
125 PRINT"■OF COURSES."
126 PRINT"■AND SEE WHICH SUIT"
127 PRINT"■YOU BEST":BA=1
128 FORV=1TO6000:NEXT:PO=7748:GOTO609
222 PRINT"○"
223 PRINT"SEE GOOD JOB BOOK"
224 PRINT"■ANU LIST OF EMPLOYERS"
225 GOSUB1000
226 BA=2:FORV=1TO6000:NEXT:PO=8150:GOTO609
250 PRINT"○       MAP INDEX"
251 PRINT"■1.PROSPECTUSES"
252 PRINT"2.SPONSORSHIPS"
253 PRINT"3.D.E.S BOOKS"
254 PRINT"4.CAREER PROFILES"
255 PRINT"5.BOX FILE"
256 PRINT"6.HOW TO DECIDE"
257 PRINT"■WHICH ONE ?"
258 GETNO:IFNO=0THEN258
259 ONNOGOTO601,602,603,604,605,606
600 GOTO250
601 PO=7748:GOTO609
602 PO=7814:GOTO609
603 PO=8100:GOTO609
```

```
604 PO=8150:GOTO609
605 PO=8156:GOTO609
606 PO=7756:GOTO609
609 PRINT"⬛";
610 PRINT
611 PRINT"▓▓▓       ▓▓▓▓▓▓▓▓▓▓▓▓▓▓▓▓▓";
612 PRINT"▓▓▓       ▓▓▓▓▓▓▓▓▓▓▓▓▓▓▓▓▓";
613 PRINT"▓▓▓       ▓▓▓▓▓▓▓▓▓▓▓▓▓▓▓▓▓";
614 PRINT"▓▓▓▓▓     ▓▓▓▓▓▓▓▓▓▓▓▓▓▓▓▓▓";
615 PRINT"▓▓▓▓▓     ▓▓▓▓▓▓▓▓▓▓▓▓▓▓▓▓▓";
616 PRINT"▓▓▓▓▓                     ";
617 PRINT"▓▓▓▓▓▓                    ";
618 PRINT"▓▓▓▓▓▓                    ";
619 PRINT"▓▓▓▓▓▓                    ";
620 PRINT"▓▓▓▓▓▓                    ";
621 PRINT"▓▓▓▓▓▓                    ";
622 PRINT"▓▓▓▓▓▓                    ";
623 PRINT"▓▓▓▓▓                     ";
624 PRINT"▓▓▓                       ";
625 PRINT"▓▓▓                       ";
626 PRINT"▓▓▓                       ";
627 PRINT"▓▓▓                       ";
628 PRINT"▓▓▓                       ";
629 PRINT"▓▓▓      ▓▓▓▓▓▓▓▓▓▓▓       ";
630 PRINT"▓▓▓▓  ▓▓▓▓▓▓▓▓▓▓▓▓▓▓▓     ";
631 PRINT"▓▓▓▓▓▓▓▓▓▓▓▓▓▓▓▓▓▓▓       ";
633 FORX=1TO20:POKEPO,81:FORC=1TO100:NEXTC:POKEPO,87:FORC=1TO100:NEXTC,X
634 PRINT"▓▓▓▓▓▓▓▓▓▓▓▓▓▓▓HIT A SPACE▓"
635 GOSUB100
636 IFBA=1THEN1008
637 IFBA=2THEN1508
638 IFBA=3THEN2008
640 GOTO10
1000 PRINT"⬛,CAREERS 84/85"
1001 PRINT"⬛,COIC CAREERS PROFILES"
1002 PRINT"⬛FOR :-"
1003 PRINT"RANGE NATURE TRAINING"
1004 PRINT"LOCATION PROSPECTS"
1005 PRINT"LIFESTYLE"
1006 RETURN
1008 PRINT"⬛";A$
1009 PRINT"⬛THEN SEE UNIVS' POLYS'";
1010 PRINT"AND COLLEGES'"
1011 PRINT"PROSPECTUSES FOR:-"
1012 PRINT"CONTENT"
1013 PRINT"NATURE OF INSTITUTIONS";
1014 PRINT"LOCATION"
1015 PRINT"TEACHING METHODS"
1016 PRINT"ACCOMMODATION"
1017 PRINT"AND FACILITIES":PRINT"▓▓HIT A SPACE"
1018 POKE198,0:WAIT198,1:POKE198,0
1019 BA=3:PO=7790:GOTO609
1508 PRINT"⬛";A$
1509 PRINT"GO BACK TO SIGNPOSTS"
1510 PRINT"TO CONSIDER POSSIBLE"
1511 PRINT"ALTERNATIVES,OR"
1512 PRINT"GAIN MORE INFORMATION"
1513 PRINT"▓HIT A SPACE":POKE198,0:WAIT198,1:POKE198,0
1514 BA=0:GOTO609
2008 PRINT"⬛";A$
2009 PRINT"NOW CONSIDER GRADUATE"
2010 PRINT"DESTINATIONS"
2011 PRINT"⬛SEE"
2012 PRINT"WHAT GRADUATES DO'"
2013 PRINT"          AND"
2014 PRINT"GRADUATE STATISTICS"
2015 PRINT"HIT A SPACE":POKE198,0:WAIT198,1:POKE198,0
2016 PO=7759:BA=0:GOTO609
READY.
```